My Times, My Town

All the best Laura —

[signature]

Other books by Walt Bodine

What Do You Say to That?

Right Here in River City
(with Tracy Thomas)

My Times, My Town

Walt Bodine

KANSAS CITY STAR BOOKS
KANSAS CITY, MISSOURI

Published by KANSAS CITY STAR BOOKS
1729 Grand Boulevard, Kansas City, Missouri 64108

First Edition

Library of Congress Card Number: 2003113747

ISBN 0-9746012-4-1

Printed in the United States of America
by Walsworth Publishing Co.
Marceline, Missouri

Book Design
Jean Donaldson Dodd

C O N T E N T S

DEDICATION

When the children of the Bodine family were growing up, I used to wonder how they'd be affected by having a father who was in the spotlight on both television and radio. Would they be tempted to bask a little in the spotlight themselves? Or would they do the opposite and seek normal lives? I am very proud that they chose the latter.

I am less proud of myself. I missed too much of their growing-up time because I thought it was necessary to have a successful career. When a big story broke, my chair at the dinner table usually was empty. Other times, I might have been at home but apart from the family, toiling over details of a newsroom budget or some other necessity of the moment. For this I apologize to them — right here, right now. Furthermore, I give them thanks and I want to honor them. Coming through it all, they were very normal and natural kids, and now they are that way as adults.

This book, then, is dedicated with all my heart to my family — my wife, Bernie, my sons, Marty, Tom and Damien, and my daughters, Mary and Rebecca.

ACKNOWLEDGMENTS

My special thanks go to the editor of this book, Monroe Dodd of *The Kansas City Star*, who is dedicated to getting things right — down to the last detail. At the same time he is a friendly, affable man with a sense of humor and a reassuring manner that served well every time I began to wonder whether this book ever would make it.

If you come away liking this book, remember the name Kay Wallick. This volume would not exist without her. She found a way for a blind man to dictate his story on a small, handheld tape recorder, and then set up machinery at her home with which she translated it all into neat pages of copy. Kay, who years ago was the producer of one of my shows on WHB, handled this task until work commitments required more of her time. By then the book was no longer an impossibility. Marty Bodine, my oldest son, volunteered to help finish some of the writing, editing, typing and other chores. It was not an easy task.

There was also the contribution of Karen Stubbs, executive director of the Kansas City branch of Coro. She rendered valuable assistance in the final phases of the project, helping re-read the book, page by page, chapter by chapter, and providing valuable last-minute insights.

x

FOREWORD

B efore you jump into this adventure, you should know that 60 years is a long time in any career. My life in broadcasting has been sometimes funny, sometimes dangerous, and often just plain crazy. In this business doubt is constant, and the ground shifts as you struggle to keep up with changes in the profession and in the world you're covering. It can be humbling. Once a boy came up to me and asked for an autograph. I signed, and he asked for a second autograph, and then a third.

"Why do you need so many?" I asked.

"I really need five," he replied, "because I can trade five Walt Bodines for one Len Dawson."

This book covers a lot of years, so forgive me if sometimes it's missing exact dates or certain details. What's important is what happened and what it meant. My life has seen a wide variety of amusing incidents, and some unsettling ones, too. In broadcasting, "security" means that you've made it through the day without major screw-ups — or without major changes, such as when a new owner takes over, or a consultant decides your fate.

After working for 10 radio and four television stations, in tenures ranging from a week to 20 years, I can tell you that it has been a good ride. I hope that it will make a good read.

CHAPTER I

The Trauma of Grade School - Tree-Sitting - The Isis Theatre -
Hard Times on the Streets - Bullies - Getting Even -
Success at Last

Before my parents met, my mother, Mary Ethel Gilmore, and her sister, Maudie, worked in dime stores in downtown Kansas City. They played piano for people who were shopping for sheet music and who wanted to know how it sounded. They both worked on Main Street — my mother for Kresge's and my aunt for Woolworth's.

My father, Walton Bodine, a pharmacist at a store at 12th and Oak, wandered over to 12th and Main on his lunch hour to enjoy the music. That's where he met my mother. Later, my father enrolled at the Conservatory of Music with a plan in mind for them to become a musical duo, she on the piano and he on the violin. It didn't work out. As he told the story, he never learned anything except how to hold a bow.

The rest, including me, is history.

———————————

I was an only child. Only in kindergarten did I discover that I wasn't the center of the universe. Years later I saw a bumper sticker that summed up what I learned: "You are a unique individual...and so is everybody else."

1

For kindergarten, I attended the old Hyde Park school at 34th and Kenwood in midtown.   Armour Boulevard was a posh area where well-to-do folks lived, and many sent their children to Hyde Park. One of my classmates — a boy with long, curly, blond hair — arrived at school every day in a car driven by a chauffeur. I've often wondered where that boy is today.

In kindergarten we had naptime but it was a futile effort. As instructed, everybody put their heads down on their folded arms. To this day, I am convinced that not one child ever fell asleep. Before long, you would work your head up a little bit, peeking around to see who might be peeking back. Sometimes it was the teacher. You couldn't win them all.

For me, grade school was a continual trauma. In the first grade I attended Prescott School in Kansas City, Kansas. A highlight was May Day.   The teacher trotted us out to the playground, where we formed a circle around the maypole and practiced for the May Day dance.   That was when I first encountered problems with coordination. Time after time after time I went the wrong way around the maypole or got my ribbon twisted up with somebody else's. The teacher stopped short of yelling at me, but I knew that I was probably causing her to lose sleep.

When the day of the big event arrived I was determined to do it right. All the parents were in the audience waiting proudly for their children to perform. Things didn't go well. Before the May Day dance was over I had managed to go the wrong way, get twisted up with several other people and finally pull the maypole halfway to the ground before someone righted it.

After that incident and a few others, I was happy that we were moving back to Missouri. I could start over in the second grade at Longfellow School, where there were no maypoles.

No place in Kansas City represents my childhood better than Longfellow. To this day when I pass it, I reflect on my time there in the late 1920s and early 1930s and give thanks that life has been much better since those painful years.

At Longfellow, when kids gathered in the schoolyard to choose up sides for baseball, Donald the fat boy and I had the distinction of being the last two chosen. The team captains would say: "*I* had to take them last time. *You* take them this time." It is not easy to come to grips with the fact that you are not an asset to the team. Perhaps it was because I was the runt of the litter, and nearsighted to boot. I could not see a ball coming and, when I did, I was more inclined to duck than try to catch it.

This and other things contributed to my longstanding dislike of athletics — and gymnasium classes in particular. I remember the glee with which my comrades, arms stretched out, headed for the hour in the gym. I dragged along behind with Donald the fat boy. The two of us dreaded that hour as much as our compatriots loved it. We referred to the gym teacher — behind his back, of course — as The Gorilla.

Today, I'm told, gym classes have changed. If someone is not good at games and exercises, special efforts are made to help him or her feel successful. That was not The Gorilla's theory. He believed that if you were no good you needed to be humbled.

Session after session I came to terms with my inadequacy.

When we high-jumped they kept lowering the bar until I could get over. For Donald the fat boy, they didn't even try. On the most horrible day of all, we entered the gym and saw long ropes dangling from the high ceiling almost to the floor. What on earth were those for? A sickening feeling grew in my stomach. The Gorilla called us out in alphabetical order. Our task was to climb a rope — all the way to the top of the ceiling.

Some of my classmates illustrated their monkey-like qualities by the speed with which they grasped the rope and climbed, hand over hand. At the top they swung on the rope, laughing and shouting to their friends. All the while, I was down below, just trying to figure out how to get my feet up on the thing. Once that was accomplished, I couldn't figure out how to climb. Though I tried over and over, I couldn't get up the rope. Finally I sensed a presence. There, looking down at me, was The Gorilla.

"What's the trouble here?"

"I can't climb the rope."

"What do you mean you can't climb the rope?"

There was little to be gained by talking further to an adult who couldn't understand a simple sentence. The Gorilla got the last word and I ended up doing 50 pushups, carefully counted out by a classmate who also happened to be my worst enemy.

Outside school the adventures were more exciting. About the time I was in the third grade I fell in with a fad that was sweeping the city — tree-sitting. People climbed trees in their yards and came down only for restroom breaks. Food was hoisted to them on a rope. Spectators came from all around just to look up to see who was in a tree.

"How long you going to stay up there?" they'd yell, and the person in the tree would yell back: "Maybe forever. I don't know." To me it seemed very cool. The local record-holder lived near 31st and Indiana. My family drove there and stood in a crowd under the champion's tree. He didn't say much; only waving once in a while. If you were one of the lucky ones who knew him, he'd call you by name. It was exciting to be standing next to someone who actually knew the tree-sitter.

I persuaded a couple of friends who lived nearby, Kenneth and Donald Ferg, to join me in a large tree in our backyard. We climbed up and, at a nice juncture of large branches, Donald and Kenneth made themselves at home. I climbed up a little farther. We were enjoying the breeze. After about 30 minutes we began to ask, "When does something happen?"

Suddenly, one of them said, "Hey, there's a white thousand-legger coming down the tree behind you!" I was never one for millipedes and I had heard that if a thousand-legger stung you with its poison you would die. Equally horrifying was the thought that this was an *albino* thousand-legger. Lord knows what damage it could do!

I whirled around quickly to try to knock it off the limb, but even before I could lay eyes on it I lost my balance, and down I went. As I neared the ground I stuck my left arm in front of me, and as I hit I heard a sound like the breaking of a stalk of celery. Until that moment it had never occurred to me that I could be injured. Bad things happened to people — but to other people, not me. Suddenly I was confronted by reality. I looked at my arm. Instead of bending only at the wrist, it also bent in the middle of the forearm.

I ran into the house shouting: "I broke my arm! I broke my arm!" Mother sat me on the couch with a pillow under my arm and called my father to take me to the family doctor. We went downtown to the Argyle Building on 12th Street, where the doctor put me in a chair and said, "You sure did; you broke this arm." He took my wrist and pulled it out with a strong jerk so that the bones lined up end to end. Once more I had a full-length arm, but the shock was horrible and the pain intense.

Then the doctor said that it wasn't quite right. He would have to do it again.

I let out a mighty, unending scream. That convinced my parents that it should be left alone. The doctor agreed. He wrapped the arm and put it in a sling. Later, when I returned to have the wrappings removed, I almost fainted from the rush of cool air on my arm. From all that, I learned that I was as vulnerable as anyone else to pain and anguish.

While my arm was healing, people would ask, "How'd you do that?" and I would have to say, "I fell out of a tree." The lesson: If you are inclined to be awkward, stay out of precarious places. As for the albino thousand-legger, it took complete command of the tree.

Many years later I broke my arm in the parking lot of a restaurant on Broadway. I went inside and got change to use a pay phone. Someone came to pick me up and take me to the emergency room at Baptist Hospital. This time the doctors gave me an anesthetic while they set the arm. They told my wife I should remain overnight. In the middle of the night I awoke and saw a beautiful face framed with long golden hair. "Hello, I'm Angel," this vision said. For a long minute I was sure that I was about to be transported from this earth. If that had to be, at least it would be with very good-looking company. My angel went on to explain that she was a nurse and that was her name, Angel. It all came back to me that I was there for a broken arm. She began those nursing conversations: "Are you comfortable? Could I bring you a glass of water?" That broke the heavenly spell.

During my grade school years, I published a weekly newspaper about happenings around the neighborhood. I would print it by hand on a piece of paper and take it to the subscribers, who gave me a penny to read it — one subscriber at a time. After a customer read it, I snatched it back and moved on to the next.

My best story came from an older kid who told me about a giant bird that lurked in the trees in our neighborhood. Every now and then, my source said, the bird dived toward earth to pick something up with its giant claws. That was big news. I rushed it to all of my subscribers and followed it up with stories supplied by my friend. One headline read, "Giant Bird Swoops Down and Snatches Dog." Having no way to substantiate that other than my friend's assurances, I was forced to end the coverage of the giant bird. After a brief few weeks as the owner and editor of this one-copy newspaper, I ceased publication.

When I was in fourth grade we moved from 28th and Harrison to 3023 Charlotte. One hot summer day I persuaded my mother to let me take two orange crates out to the curb with a pitcher of lemonade and some cups, and sell drinks to passersby. Sitting on one orange crate and selling lemonade from the other, I was positioned directly in front of my house where potential customers couldn't miss me as they walked past. Even cars stopped once in a while, and the drivers whistled me over to bring them a cup in exchange for a nickel. There I was, busily serving my clientele, when an old gentleman came along.

"Well, young fellow, how's business today?" he asked.

"Just fine. A nickel a cup for fresh lemonade."

Instead of buying, he asked, "How are you doing so far?" and I began to realize that he was interviewing me just to pass the time of day. He certainly didn't look like a reporter. In the time he was talking, I was losing business. People who might have stopped instead glanced and moved on. I'm sure they were thinking, Who knows how long it might take the old boy to buy something — or leave?

Finally, the old man said, "Well, I don't have any change today."

"I can change a buck," I replied, hopefully.

"No," he said, "I don't have any money, but I can tell you this: you certainly have my moral support." That day I learned moral support often is supplied by people who have no intention of doing you any real good.

In the late 1920s and early 1930s, the center for entertainment in the neighborhood where I grew up was the Isis Theatre at 31st Street and Troost Avenue. It had everything: action, thrills, adventure, Betty Boop cartoons, and the weekly meeting on Saturdays of the Brer Fox Club. The manager came out to talk to the kids at each movie about next week's "giveaway." It could be a small car, even one powered with a battery, that you could ride around on your own sidewalk. Or it might be a sidewalk bike, or a large bicycle. We, the loyal members of the Brer Fox Club, believed that the prize inevitably went to a member of the manager's family. We always arrived hoping our number would be drawn, and we cherished our conspiracy theory no matter who won and no matter what he looked like. After all, the winner was never anyone that we knew.

I learned a lot at the Isis Theatre. A scary movie could follow you around for weeks afterward. I remember seeing a version of the "Phantom of the Opera" in which a man and a woman were in the upper section of a theater and the man announced that he had to leave and would be back. That often happened in the middle of a scary movie — men abandoned their women and a monster promptly appeared. In this movie, the man left a woman sitting at a table. She stood up, walked to a bureau and picked up a package of cigarettes. She removed one cigarette, turned around, and as she was lighting it, the top drawer of the bureau opened and an ugly, bony hand began to reach for her. Just then she decided to walk over and sit down at the table again. The hand quickly withdrew. But not from my fantasies.

For some time thereafter, I didn't want to go near a chest of drawers for any reason. Was it even possible for a person with a bony hand to live in a single drawer? Who knew, but why take chances?

The Isis Theatre had two balconies, both bending gracefully toward the stage. In another movie about death and torment, there was a scene in which a group of people standing in the aisle of a theater were mystified by something that had just happened. Suddenly a woman in the group looked up and let out a shrill scream. The camera panned upward and there in the balcony, looking down at them, stood a man that everyone had seen die in a movie earlier. We in the audience knew he had been dead for months. For years afterward, I could not look up toward the top balcony of the Isis because I just knew "he" was up there. I refused to acknowledge him.

We used our small allowances to get into the movies and buy candy and popcorn for 10 or 15 cents. My friend Jon Yost was the envy of all of the neighborhood kids because of his large allowance of $3.50 a week.

One day we were disappointed by a movie. It was a comedy that may have been a little too sophisticated for small boys. Across the aisle and a couple of rows back from us sat a large man who looked as if he might have just come in from the farm. He thought the movie was quite funny. He laughed, loudly at first, and then louder. It seemed he was going to collapse into the aisle from sheer exhaustion. My pal and I looked back disapprovingly. We had paid good money for a show we didn't like and had to bear the laughter of this buffoon. We began to fake laughter in hopes that his would end soon.

Now and then a touch of real showbiz glamour came to the Isis. A visiting movie star would appear for three or four minutes on stage, say something harmless and leave. We clapped hard, anyway, because there he was, a guy from the movies!

Gym class was only one of my trials at Longfellow School. There was another torture chamber, shop class, otherwise known as manual training. Instruction was minimal. The teacher spoke through his nose quickly and softly and reviewed all the objects we would be building, briefly explaining two or three of the tools we would use. I was just beginning to understand the first one when he finished the last one. We were supposed to know innately how to do the project, a simple one, building a pair of bookends.

We'd begin with a piece of wood, the teacher explained, and smooth its surface with a plane. We held a T-square on the plane to see whether any light seeped through. If none did, the wood was smooth enough. Everyone else found it simple. They went at it with their planes and in no time almost everyone had planed a piece of wood and checked it with a T-square. Even my ally, Donald, who joined me in my revulsion at gym class, seemed to do well in shop. Yet despite the kind aid of a fellow student, Hymie, a speck of light showed through mine every time I checked. By the second session I was still working on this first-session task.

I wished someone could explain planing in a way I could understand. The teacher clearly disliked me, so I didn't want to ask him. Finally, when I had planed my piece of wood down to the thickness of a couple of toothpicks, I went to the teacher to ask for another board. Why? he asked, and I showed him the old one. He grunted, and gave me a replacement. "Get it done," he said. "You need to go on to the next project." That was the first of several boards he handed to me.

At the end of the semester, we were supposed to bring our work to the teacher's desk, placing it there so he could give us a grade. As one student after another took his project to be judged I sat waiting in terror for the moment when he called me.

"All right, Bodine," he said.

I went forward and placed before him a half set of bookends. For those who have never built bookends, you are supposed to hollow out a little bit of the bottom and pour hot lead in it. That's to weight the bookend so it will stand on its own.

"Where's the other one?" the teacher asked.

"I just got one done."

"In a whole semester this is what you did?" There was laughter from all sides of the room.

"You are going to destroy the record of this school," he said. "I don't believe any boy has ever failed manual training. But if you can put that thing in front of me standing up and if it looks to be good enough I will give you an 'I' (for "inferior") instead of an 'F'." With a shaking hand I reached over and put the bookend in front of him. He stared down at it and it began to quiver. Because I had not put enough lead in the bottom, it fell over. The class roared with laughter. The teacher, who never made eye contact with me again, picked up my card and wrote a big "F" on it. I'm sure he was thinking to himself, There goes history. All I cared about was never having to go back in that room.

The next semester I had drama class and performed in the school play. Now I was in my element. Unlike gym or shop, I was the one that went dashing enthusiastically to the back stage of the theater where we assembled. So eager was I that one day I unwisely sped past the boys' restroom when I should have gone in. Once backstage, they kept us busy reading lines. I waited and at a moment in which everyone was on the stage except me, I could hold it no longer. I created a puddle on the floor that was obvious to my returning schoolmates.

"Hey, look," they cried. "Walton wet his pants!"

After 1929 we saw adults worrying about the Depression, but most of the kids took it in stride. We accepted the fact that there were things we couldn't do, and fashioned our own recreation. One way was to get our hands on a streetcar pass, which you could use to ride all day long on any line in the city. Sometimes we'd beg passes from people coming home from work for the weekend. They were good until midnight Saturday.

On the route downtown on Main Street, we could see raw evidence of what bad economic times did to human beings. At points men in tacky clothes lined both sides of the street. Sometimes they raised their fists or spat at the streetcar. Most of them simply looked defeated. You realized what it must be like to be cast out with no demand for your talents.

In the 500 block of Main the streetcar passed the Portland Hotel, a large flophouse. There was a marquee out front advertising "25 cents a night" and as an inducement "electric light in every room." There used to be a joke that you could sleep there for 25 cents — or a dollar if you wanted a clean room. One trip through that melancholy scene made you eager for the streetcar to head back south. There was a depression uptown also, but uptown was better at concealing wounds.

Down in the North End beside the Portland Hotel, there were places where a cheap bottle of wine could be had. An old policeman that I knew for years, Joe Trabon, once told me about how men sat on the back side of billboards and got so drunk they'd fall off. Now and then, he said, a man fell on his back and passed out with his eyes wide open staring straight at the sun. If that went on for long, the man could be blinded.

At night, the North End was a little more dangerous. A man could go to sleep in a doorway trying to keep warm, wake up and find that his shoes had been stolen. You've heard the expression, "They're playing hardball." I saw the real meaning of "hardball" on lower Main Street and the umpire had counted all of those men "out."

At Longfellow, I did quite well academically until I found out that other kids in the school considered me rich. My father owned a drugstore on Troost and Linwood and our family name flashed in lights on a neon sign. It didn't take much to be considered rich once the Depression was under way.

Because of my classmates' perception that my family had money, combined with my success in the classroom, some of the bullies began to threaten me on the way home from school. After a few of those episodes, I changed my approach to mediocrity in the classroom. I wanted to blend in with the other kids.

That didn't always work. In the sixth grade, Allan, a good friend of mine, was waiting for me in the schoolyard. I came out wearing a brand new cap my mother had bought me. At that moment, Allan turned tormenter. He reached over, grabbed my new hat and rubbed it in the dirt. I do not know what came over me, but I gave him a great punch — straight up and into his chin — and he fell over. I grabbed the cap, put it on and headed for home. About halfway there, as I crossed Campbell Street, it occurred to me that I might have killed him. I'd be sent to Boonville for reform school!

I went home and hid out in my room. When the doorbell rang I was sure it was the cops coming after me, but instead it was the cleaning man. Nevertheless, I knew it was only a matter of time. Maybe I should just take off running as fast as I could, I thought, and get across the state line. But then again, maybe Allan was OK. So I called his house and listened carefully to his mother's voice to determine whether she had been crying.

"Is Allan there?" I asked, and his mother said, "Yes, I'll get him, just a moment."

"Never mind," I said, "and goodbye." Allan and I resumed being friends after that and never mentioned the matter again.

What my classmates didn't understand was that the Bodine

family struggled as much as anyone else. As family members lost their jobs, their homes, and their farms, we found positions for them at the drugstore. Dollars were stretched during the Depression, yet somehow we got through.

As for my newfound academic mediocrity, I succeeded admirably until grade seven. That year, my final one at Longfellow, I began working harder than ever on my schoolwork. The hormones were taking over. Like the other boys, I noticed if my teacher happened to be pretty, and took special notice on days she wore a sweater.

For Miss Swenson, I wanted to make good grades. And I did. My reward was to be chosen to give a speech the night of graduation. My topic was "Initiative." I wrote the speech carefully and revised it a time or two. Miss Swenson made a few changes.

On the fateful night I stood up, with my parents there and an auditorium full of people. My classmates were behind me. As I started to deliver my speech, I looked out over all those faces in the audience and stopped dead in my tracks. I had no idea where I was going next.

Just then I looked down and caught the eye of my wonderful teacher. She looked at me and mouthed the words that I needed to get started. I made it through, and the audience clapped politely. The next day before leaving, I asked Miss Swenson to sign my small grade-school yearbook. She wrote, "May you always face the world with the same courage you showed last night."

Finally, there on my last day at Longfellow School, my self-esteem soared to the top.

Decades later, imagine my surprise when Longfellow reached its 100th anniversary and I was called upon to speak at a gathering in the auditorium. I thought it through carefully and wrote a great speech with great humor. By returning to the scene of long-ago humiliations, I thought, I could finally put things right. When the time came, I stood up, made it to the podium without falling, began speaking and waited for laughs. There were many laughs, right when I wanted them. I had touched a chord.

So there it was at last. The scales were balanced at Longfellow.

I received a big round of applause, turned, waved and headed for the stairs. This must have been what it was like to be Franklin Roosevelt, acknowledging an ovation after a stirring speech.

The stairs, however, were not where I thought they were. I plunged straight off the platform and landed in a belly-flop on the floor. People came running. Everything was all right, I assured them. I rose, dusted off and left.

Once out the door, I thought: "I've bombed again at Longfellow. I'm jinxed here."

This is how it went for me at Longfellow School, both early in my life and many years later. In truth, it was a good school with good teachers. But I'll have the good sense to stay out of the place from now on. Nowadays, every time I pass Longfellow School, I hope that every student there is doing better than I did.

INTERLUDE

A Lifelong Feast

I've always been devoted to food.

In kindergarten at Hyde Park school, whenever we weren't having to put our heads down and pretend to sleep, or to play some game only the teachers loved, we'd be lined up and led to a place where we received a couple of graham crackers and a bottle of milk with a straw inserted in the top. As the years went by, this became one of my favorite concoctions and it still is. Here's the recipe: Dip graham crackers two by two into a glass of milk, and jam them into your mouth before they fall apart.

In the third grade at Longfellow, a sensual reward for being in school was the brown paper sack that held my lunch. There's something I love about the smell of a brown paper sack, especially if it also smells of bananas or a ham sandwich. On warm days we were allowed to go outside with our sack lunches. On cold days we sat around in the basement.

At the beginning of one school year, I came into contact with a cafeteria for the first time, and realized

that some of what was served there was pretty good.
After collecting a tray and napkin, it was exciting to
stroll down the line and view the fare for the day.
My favorite was chipped beef on mashed potatoes.

*   *   *

Chocolate malts have been a lifelong love affair.
I had my first one when we still lived in Kansas City,
Kansas, and Dad had a drugstore at Ninth and
Minnesota. I can remember his showing me a menu
with a picture on the front of a football player kicking
a football. He opened the menu and pointed to
malts. That's what you want to try, he said. He
made me a chocolate malt and that began my
addiction. At the time you could get a plain malt for
about 10 cents. For the affluent, Dad had a super
malt with whipped cream on top for 20 cents. For a
raw egg in addition to that, you paid a nickel extra.

*   *   *

In the Depression there was another delight.
For a nickel you could get a 3Musketeers. That was a
single package with three chocolate bars inside —
one vanilla, one chocolate and one strawberry. Each
was almost as large as the single bar to which
3Musketeers has been reduced today.

*   *   *

On cold nights the tamale cart came along with its bell ringing, and kids ran out hoping to get their parents to spring for some tamales. If you succeeded, the man would take your order and then pop the top off his pushcart. A wonderful aroma spread from it. He'd wrap your tamales in plain paper and off you'd go.

CHAPTER II

At the Crossroads - Bodine's Drug Store -
Our Neighborhood - The Roar of the Fire Truck - Our Competition -
Spanish Fly - A Drive on the Wild Side - Coming of Age -
First Kiss - Wide-Eyed at the Movies

Growing up, I spent a lot of time at my father's drugstore on the corner of Linwood Boulevard and Troost Avenue. To me and my friends, that was the crossroads of America. Two major highways intersected right there. U.S. 40, on its way from the Atlantic Coast to California, traveled along Linwood. U.S. 71, headed north and south across the central United States, followed Troost. Our store was on the southwest corner.

There was a neon sign above it with the name, "Bodine." Often we set out a signboard with a picture of a strawberry sundae with whipped cream — 10 cents. Inside there was a long soda fountain, eight tables that could hold four people each and 10 booths. This substantial food business not only brought in revenue, but also provided employment for relatives who had lost their jobs or, in one case, had lost a farm.

That was the 1930s, when the Great Depression enveloped America and Kansas City. Those were my coming-of-age years, and the neighborhood where I spent them was exciting, intriguing and vastly different from the way it is today.

Here is a walking tour of my part of town as it was then —
buildings, streets, spirit and all. Catercorner from Bodine's All
Night Drug Store was a big Firestone tire store, which did a lot of
business in those days. Just up Troost was a bingo establishment
called Troost Tango, one of many that made Kansas City the Las
Vegas of that era. On the southeast corner stood the Elsmere
Hotel, on a site now dominated by a portrait of Dr. Martin Luther
King Jr. Bodine's drugstore, one story tall, extended from the
corner of the Ormond Hotel out to the sidewalk. The Ormond was
a quiet hostelry of five floors with a nice dining room inside. The
hotel's entrance on Linwood was flanked by a porch just above
sidewalk level. Hotel guests could sit there evenings and watch
the traffic and the people go by. Linwood Boulevard was quite
busy in those days, and I've watched a lot of TV and seen a lot of
movies that were less entertaining than an evening spent on the
Ormond porch.

To the west and down the hill on Linwood stood the LaSalle
Hotel, now razed. At one time, it was a large, handsome hotel
topped by a neon sign that could be read blocks away.

Things just seemed to happen at the LaSalle. One night I was
awakened by the sound of machine-gun fire. The mob was
rubbing out a couple of errant brethren who were trying to get
away through a side door. On another occasion, I was walking
down the hill on Linwood and came upon a cluster of people
standing under the LaSalle marquee. Just then sirens sounded,
and a couple of police motorcycles came around the corner
escorting a limousine containing baseball's favorite of the
moment, Dizzy Dean, and his brother, Paul.

Farther west on Linwood you came to the Kansas City Athenaeum, frequented by well-heeled ladies who gathered for civic projects. I loved to watch as they arrived for luncheon, a few in genteel electric cars that traveled about 15 miles an hour. Some of those cars could be operated by a stick from the back seat. Inside, the car looked like an atrium that grew old ladies. We kids didn't really know what went on in the Athenaeum, but because of the cars and the building we assumed that it was "rich" stuff.

On the south side of Linwood were more apartment buildings, and here and there a house. We marveled about one house on the corner of Linwood and Charlotte where there was an endless parade of cars. They parked in front of the house for short periods, drove away and were replaced by more cars. Almost everyone who went in was male. We could speculate about what went on in there, and figured it probably was naughty. That appealed strongly to young boys.

Across the street from that house was a Seventh Day Adventist Church, where people came on Saturday all dressed for worship. Farther west along the block was a non-union cleaning shop. One night — as I sat at the table in our apartment working on my homework, a rare thing for me — came the terrific noise of an explosion. I looked up in time to see the whole cleaning shop blown out into the street. Afterward, I wondered how many people would want the operator to pay for their destroyed clothes.

And there was Feinberg Kosher Delicatessen, a source of great interest. We could go in with a single nickel and get a little spear to fish a kosher dill pickle from a barrel. The clerk wrapped it in a napkin and we walked away eating it like an ice cream cone.

We liked watching the rabbi oversee preparations. He was an impressive figure with his black clothing and black beard and hat. At Feinberg I also learned the wonderful taste of kosher franks.

Across Linwood from all that was the big Delmar Apartment building, which extended from 712 to 718 Linwood. My parents and I moved a lot during the Depression and at various times we lived in three different apartments in that building. Often, someone would knock and say, "If you want to move out of this place when your lease is up, you can come over to our place and your first six months will be free."

Next door to us was a house where a kind, mustachioed gentleman owned a radio store. He was a nice old man who'd sit on the front porch and chat with us. The kids in the neighborhood, however, found that if we went around and peered into his basement at night we'd see men go in. Our elderly friend would greet them, pick up a syringe and give them a shot in the arm. We never told anyone because we didn't know what we were looking at, though we were pretty sure it was illegal. One day the feds moved in. It was one of the first times that I picked up *The Kansas City Star* and saw a story I knew about personally.

In the Depression, children were conscious that their parents couldn't afford any pricey entertainments, so we invented our own games. On a typical hot summer day we might start with hide-and-seek. Later we'd talk the apartment janitor into bringing out the garden hose and spraying us in our bathing suits. Our favorite perch was the front steps, where we never tired of watching an endless procession of cars, buses and emergency vehicles on Linwood Boulevard. From what I recall, I never heard a child in those days come out with a petulant, "I'm bored."

Our heroes were the men from Fire Station No. 17 on Holmes between 30th and 31st streets, where there was a fire chief, a pumper truck and a hook-and-ladder truck. When we heard the external alarm go off a block away, we'd dash to the corner of Linwood and Holmes to watch the firefighters roar past. First came the chief and his driver, then the pumper truck, the old-fashioned kind where firemen hung on as they stood on a platform at the rear. Finally, the hook-and-ladder truck rounded the corner, looking ungainly as always.

We liked to walk over to visit the station. Early on, the firemen told us: "You can come up and see us any time, but notice the orange painted line that goes around all of the fire trucks. You can't go beyond that. When an alarm sounds we don't have time to go looking for kids standing in the way."

Once in a while the alarm rang while we were there. Amid the clanging, the dispatcher yelled out an address over the PA system. With a roar the big motors revved up. The trucks rolled into the street, sirens blaring, and quickly passed out of earshot. Suddenly, the place that had been so busy and noisy had an eerie calm.

Another source of excitement was the ambulance corps of General Hospital at 24th and Holmes. Many of their runs took them down Holmes to Linwood and then east or west. The ambulances were panel trucks with windows in the back. Sometimes we could catch a glimpse of the patient through them.

One exciting night, we were sitting out front when an ambulance approached on Holmes going faster than usual. When the driver turned left onto Linwood, the ambulance jumped the curb onto the sidewalk. That jolted the back doors open — and out rolled the wheeled cot. Luckily for all, no one was on it.

We did unusual things to raise money. For people strolling along Troost on Friday and Saturday nights, we put on mock weddings in doorways of closed stores. One of us would dress like a groom, another like a minister, and another like a bride. I had been taking violin lessons — although to no great end — and my job was to play a little music to set the mood. When the ceremony was done, we'd pass the hat. Once the first crowd cleared we would begin our second wedding for the evening, and so on. On a good night, with all our efforts over several hours, we might turn $2 or $3.

We also entertained ourselves keeping track of what the car dealers were doing. We loved it when the new models were about to come out. Down on the corner of Holmes and Linwood was Newman Fox Ford, where employees soaped up the windows from the inside and then rolled the new models out on the floor. On the appointed day they opened the door and everybody came in to see the latest cars. Then they wiped the soap off the windows. We'd get there a day or so beforehand when the cars were already in place, find an opening in that soap and peek in. Then we could say, "We've seen the new Ford!" We did the same at Sight Brothers Chevrolet at 31st and Gillham as soon as they put the white stuff on the windows.

The only bad experience we had wandering the

neighborhoods was with Cleda Fern. She was a schoolmate of ours at Longfellow School and a couple of grades behind me. On an icy day on the way home from school, Cleda fell on the ice, struck her head on the curb, and died.

Dead? People our age didn't die! We were indestructible. How could it be that somebody walking to school was suddenly not part of this earth anymore? The day of her funeral, all the kids went to look down the block where she had lived, a little side street called Glenairy Place. We saw a lot of grownups wearing dark clothes, getting out of their cars and going into Cleda's house. We stood there stunned, and then one by one drifted away, thinking about the meaning of death.

Often on our street we observed a man strutting along with his wife right behind, carrying the groceries. The man would stop and, occasionally punctuating his patter by poking his finger at us, explain with great conviction the virtues of Nazi Germany and of Adolf Hitler. His wife never said anything. She would give a loyal smile if you looked at her, as if to say that underneath his bluster he was really a nice man. When he resumed his procession up the street, she followed obediently, all the while carrying all the groceries. We were told later that this man once had been a good baseball player. If he was such a good athlete, we wondered, why couldn't he have helped his wife carry the groceries?

At Linwood and Charlotte on the north side lived a gentleman we called "The Swami." He wore a turban and whenever we kids saw him coming down the street we hid behind a bush. No matter what happened, for some reason we just knew that he should not see us. We watched as he arrived at his rooming house and climbed the stairs to his room on the second floor. As we gathered behind the hedge, he went through what seemed to be a prayer ritual. When he turned in our direction we all ducked quickly.

———————————————

Linwood and Troost was a great spot for a drugstore, and Bodine's was hardly the only one in the neighborhood. There were several drugstores within two blocks. To make things worse the Katz Drugstore chain, which had large outlets all over town, supplied powerful competition. As a big company Katz could buy from wholesalers more cheaply than Bodine's could. The large Katz ads that appeared in the newspaper every few days gave my father fits. One of his solutions was to mount the latest Katz ad on a special counter with a slanting top right by the front door. On it he placed a sign: "We meet every price in this ad so save your gasoline."

Salesmanship ran in the family. My father's father, Ashby Bodine, was an early adopter of the phonograph in the 19th century. He took the machine from county fair to county fair, charging people a nickel to listen to it. According to family legend, one strange fellow decided the machine was playing devils' voices and tried to do in my grandfather. Luckily, he survived. Unhappily, much Bodine genealogy didn't survive. There would always be time, I thought, to go through the handwritten family tree my dad kept in the prescription department at the drugstore. That document, however, was destroyed one day when a fire swept through drugstore. In the single picture I've seen of

Grandfather Ashby Bodine, he had a giant mustache, twinkling eyes and what appeared to be a sense of humor. He was quite the promoter.

My Dad devoted his considerable skills not only to promotion, but also to customer service. All our neighborhood competitors delivered to the apartments and hotels nearby, especially on Linwood and Armour boulevards. The rule in Bodine's was, "No phone ever rings twice." If we didn't answer the phone before the end of the first ring my Dad would give us his look.

Uncle Willie, my father's brother, ran the place on the overnight shift from 11 p.m. until 7 a.m. One night several people were sitting at the soda fountain, many of them folks who came in to eat after the bars closed. A man entered, pulled a gun, pointed it at Uncle Willie and asked for the cash. Just then the phone by the soda fountain rang. From habit, Uncle Willie told the stickup man, "Just a minute," and raced over to answer the phone on the first ring. As he took the caller's order the holdup man stood there with his gun, no doubt thinking, "I'm the bad guy, I have a gun in my hand, and this man goes off and talks on the phone." All the customers were turning around to look at him. He put the gun back in his pocket and walked out.

Occasionally, we got notable visitors at the soda fountain. One was a budding comic named Red Skelton. He was working at the El Torreon Dance Hall as a funnyman and master of ceremonies for a Walk-A-Thon. When he finished at 1 or 2 a.m., he would come over to Bodine's, slide onto a stool, have his dinner and then go into a comedy routine. The people at the fountain listened and laughed. My Uncle Willie, who used a lot of interesting expressions learned from having lived on a farm, said, "Walton, that fellow could make a dog laugh."

Johnny Lazia, the reputed gangland leader of Kansas City in those years, was a regular customer. He had lots of business that kept him up late. In the early hours of the morning, a black limo would pull up outside the drugstore. A man would come to the door and make sure everything was OK inside, then signal. Lazia would enter and sit down at the fountain. While his men stood guard outside, he would have a short chat with Uncle Willie and a chocolate malt.

In 1934 Uncle Willie served Johnny Lazia his last meal. One summer night that year, when he finished his malt, Lazia got back into the car and was delivered to the Park Central on Armour Boulevard. As he stepped from the car, men appeared from behind bushes at the southeast corner of the building and mowed him down. Lazia died the next day. It was said that he resisted all questioning by police officers — in the gangland spirit of keeping mum.

The pharmacy room at Bodine's was barely large enough to accommodate four chairs against the south wall. They were occupied often on Friday and Saturday nights as a result of one of my father's business innovations: Selling leeches for $1 apiece. We had a big bowl of leeches on the table where the prescriptions were filled. Anyone who had been in a fight, anyone who had a blossoming black eye could come in and for $1 we would hang one of the leeches near an eye or on an eyelid or wherever the problem was, and the leech would suck away the blood and there would be no black eye. It was a pretty impressive operation. On weekend nights quite a few people took punches and they'd come in afterward. There were times when we would see all four seats filled with men in various states of drunkenness, each with a leech hanging from his eye.

One day at Bodine's I wandered into the prescription department near the soda fountain and found my cousin staring up at a locked cabinet.

"What's up?" I asked. "What are you looking at?"

"You know what's up there and why it is locked up?"

"No."

"Spanish fly, that's what."

That meant nothing to me until I was told it was a potion that, placed in drink or food, would make women sexually ravenous for you. About that time the pharmacist came in.

"Is that really the name of that stuff up there?" I asked. "Spanish fly?"

"Its real name is Tincture of Cantharides," the pharmacist replied, "and I'm busy now, so get out of here."

I first went to work behind the soda fountain at Bodine's All Night Drug Store at the age of 15. Chocolate malt fans never went away disappointed, especially my friends when they came in to visit me. They'd order a chocolate malt and I'd give them extra dips of ice cream. My father would shake his head and say, "There's not a dime's worth of profit in the soda fountain when you're on." And this super malt cost all of 20 cents.

While I worked behind the soda fountain, my strangest customer was known behind the scenes as the Blue Man. He came in at least once every day and sometimes twice to drink a Bromo Seltzer. Behind the counter we had a large, blue bottle full of tablets. We'd take a tablet or two and add it to a glass of carbonated water. Word on the street was that if you drank enough of it you began to turn blue. In the case of the Blue Man, at least, I saw that happen. The creases in his skin became dark blue and the rest of his complexion a mild blue. He was a sight to see.

The "working girls" came in every afternoon for a Coke and cigarette before heading to the nearby hotels about 5 o'clock. Most of them were busy talking to each other, but there was one who called herself Nancy Hanks who always talked to *me*. She asked me about school and my life. You can work all day in a soda fountain and feel as if you're just somebody who carries food and drinks to people who don't even look at you. But Nancy — my queen, my angel — treated me like a human being. When I got married, I told a friend, I wanted to marry someone like Nancy.

He explained to me that she was a prostitute. I had a strong desire to punch him out, left work angry, and when I went to bed that night the matter was still on my mind. When I woke up in the morning I had a sudden blast of cold truth — what my friend told me was for real. After that I could not bring myself to look Nancy in the eye. I was afraid that she would know that I knew, and I didn't want to hurt her.

One year , my father converted one corner of the store to a bus stop. The big bus stations downtown were inconvenient for many people who lived or worked a great distance away. For Bodine's, it attracted new business and also brought the store a 10 percent cut of each ticket sold. When I worked as ticket agent we sold tickets to such faraway places as Hickman Mills, Belton, and Harrisonville.

About the time I was able to borrow Dad's car, several friends and I made it an occasional adventure to drive through Kansas City's red-light district. The heart of this was 14th and Cherry, and it extended several blocks east almost to Paseo. By way of 13th Street it traced a lurid path back to Cherry. No wonder people like the newspaper columnist Westbrook Pegler referred to Kansas City as a Paris of the Prairies.

We drove through the area in the summertime with the windows rolled down, hearing the girls call: "Come on in, boys. We'll show you a good time." We kept driving, trying to act nonchalant. But our resolve was shaken when traffic jammed up. Suddenly, we were pinned. If one of the ladies of the evening came toward the car, we'd be in near panic. Suddenly confronted by reality, things became different for rambunctious teen-age boys. The minute there was an opening in the traffic we'd dart through and drive away.

When I was 16, I met a girl named Marguerite at a large family gathering. There was something about her that warmed my blood. She was pretty and bright-eyed, and we made a date before the day was out. We met weekly after that. One night we found ourselves seated on the front porch at 712 Linwood on a glider. Marguerite chatted quietly as I glanced inside and saw the adults retiring to the dining room for a game of gin rummy. Impetuous youth that I was, I thought to myself: It's now or never! I looked at her and she looked at me, and I drew her closer and kissed her.

"This is not bad!" I thought.

Would there be stars in her eyes? I pulled back to check and saw that she was merely looking at the top of my head.

"Do you know that your hair is sticking up in back?" she asked.

Future encounters with Marguerite were more romantic, but that cowlick never went away. I tried to paste it down with lots of Lucky Tiger. Boy and man, I have always had that unruly shock of hair. I've combed it in a variety of ways, and consulted endless barbers, including my current barber, Bill Shockley. One time I even had a stylist come to my house, but he finally conceded that there was no way to defeat the cowlick completely. It's been a long fight, and one I could never win. I now accept my hirsute challenge.

As the 1930s wore on, we continued to frequent the Isis Theatre. In my early teenage years, my friend Jon Yost called to say: "There's something going on at the Isis you've got to see. I've got some extra allowance. I'm going there tonight."

He wouldn't tell me what it was, but I was curious enough

to meet him. We went in and sat down.

"Now, tell me, why are we here?" I asked.

"It's in the movie with Ginger Rogers. I'll tell you when it's going to happen."

At that age, Ginger Rogers and Fred Astaire bored me but Yost assured me this would be worthwhile.

"OK, get ready; here it comes," he said. In the movie, Ginger Rogers sat on a bench and Fred Astaire approached her with some ardor.

"Look," my friend said. "Look at her chest." I suddenly realized you could see through her blouse. Just as I caught on and got really interested, the scene ended. Astaire had lured her back onto the dance floor. I want to say that we did *not* hang around the theater an hour and a half to watch the scene repeated at the next screening — but that would be telling a lie!

The Isis was a place where you discovered who you were — and what you could get away with. After junior high school, we began taking our girlfriends, trying to convince them that sitting up in the top balcony we could see better. Sometimes it worked, but often the girl was too smart to fall for it. There was an additional hazard. In those days there were ushers in movie theaters. If some couple in the balcony seemed to be having too good a time, they might be halted abruptly by an usher shining a flashlight, while people nearby snickered. The usher gave a disapproving look, and you wondered whether he was going to report you to the vice squad.

The Isis was a big part of my life. It marked many passages, and the final one came years later, when one day I passed the corner of 31st and Troost and saw that the Isis had been torn down.

It was another lesson that nothing lasts forever.

INTERLUDE

Food: Serving It, Eating It

Maybe it's because I came from a family of
restaurant people that food is so important to me.

In my father's drugstore we served soups and
sandwiches as well as sodas. That was during the
Depression, when even a nickel was an acceptable tip
— if you got any tip at all. When you found a nickel
you were tempted to run out and call to the patron,
"Did you leave your change by mistake?" One night
I was working the night shift and a friendly though
possibly inebriated gentleman came in, ate quite a lot
and left a half dollar under the plate. That was a
major happening. Fighting off the temptation to
check whether he meant to leave that much, I
hastened to make short work of the money. The next
evening he returned and said that he had left some
money by mistake and he would like to have it back.
He was too late.

*   *   *

At one time, my father and his two brothers owned three restaurants in Kansas City, diners in unpretentious neighborhoods. I used to ask my uncles and my father about people who ordered strange combinations of food. They told me about customers who wanted sugar on their steak or salt on their watermelon, and who methodically spread their pancakes with mustard. At one of the restaurants there was man who came in almost every day, ordered custard pie and then dumped catsup on it.

*   *   *

My father was forever thinking of new things to serve at the soda fountain of Bodine's. In some restaurant, he saw little finger sandwiches grouped in fours with different ingredients in each, and he wanted to try that dish at Bodine's. I told my father that some of our most important customers were cab drivers and that they wouldn't think much of little finger sandwiches. But I was wrong again. Almost to a man, the cab drivers thought they were great. They ate finger sandwiches and I ate humble pie.

CHAPTER III

Radio Days - I Faw' Down and Go Boom! - Calling Buses -
Stumbling Start on a Career - Is Anybody Out There Listening? -
The War - A Job in the City

From the time I was old enough to drive, I spent my free time in a car preparing for my radio career. I'd call out, "This is CBS, the Columbia Broadcasting System" or "This is NBC, the National Broadcasting Company." Or, I might lower myself: "This is the Mutual Broadcasting Company." Station breaks were part of the monologue: "This is WHB, Cook Paint and Varnish Company, Kansas City." In my dreams, the car was my studio and my listeners were all around. In reality, I wasn't sure what I was going to do with my life. All the while, no doubt, people in other cars were remarking about that silly guy over there talking to himself.

My first and probably worst broadcast appearance took place even before that, when I was about 8 years old. My Aunt Maude played the piano for an afternoon kiddy show at a small radio station that had a studio in the penthouse of the LaSalle Hotel. One day she brought me in to perform a popular novelty song: "I Faw Down an' Go Boom." I wasn't good with most of the lyrics, but each time the last line of the chorus came around, I could sing out, "I faw down an' go boom!" From my perspective standing on a chair, the microphone was forbidding. It was suspended inside a big ring of metal by four things that looked like rubber bands. The next day, I was impressed when the mother of one of my friends told me I had sounded great on the radio.

That may have planted the seed. By the time I became a teenager in the 1930s, I was enthralled by the medium.

My friend Jon Yost and I looked forward with great anticipation to our afternoon trips to WHB's studio in the Scarritt Building on Grand Avenue downtown. We'd go there almost every day to watch a locally produced show called "Staff Frolic." The studio audience was composed of people hard up for something to do, people who'd wait for the doors to be thrown open. "Staff Frolic" consisted of WHB staff members (I remember one named Jack Grogan and another named Les Jarvies) doing comedy skits, singing songs and generally filling the slot with impromptu entertainment. Once in a while a man with great talent played piano. Later we learned that his name was Count Basie. The Count seemed happy enough to pick up a five-spot from WHB by playing an hour show. And, although $5 may seem like peanuts in today's world, that was macadamia nuts in those days.

Yost and I became convinced that "Staff Frolic" was the daily radio fare in hundreds of thousands of homes. Surely everyone knew about the stellar performances in that small studio. In fact, one of the performers was our classmate from Westport High School, Milton Frank. Listening to his great work as a singer made us feel as if we were on the "inside" — we actually knew someone who sang on the radio.

One night at the dinner table, I said to my father, "You've heard of Milton Frank, the singer, haven't you?"

He looked up from his scalloped potatoes and ham and said, "No, can't say I have."

"You know, he's on WHB."

"I don't listen much to that station. I'm busy most of the day."

It was the best show in town, yet it had failed to win the allegiance of my father, a very bright man!

———

Not long after I graduated from high school in 1938, a tense moment took place in our living room at the apartment building on Linwood. My father asked me a question out of the blue, a question I had dreaded.

"No, Dad," I said in reply, summoning all my strength, "I don't want to go into the drugstore business. I don't want to be a pharmacist. I don't much want to be a businessman.

"I'm thinking," I went on, "of being an actor."

My father was surprised, as I thought he would be.

"That's about as hard a thing as you could pick," he said, "but if that's what you are going to do, you'd better get cracking. What are you going to do about it? Are you going to college?"

I was afraid that was going to come up. No, I didn't want to go to college. High school had been partly fun, but mostly misery. I wanted to escape from being locked in classrooms, listening to teachers drone on.

"Well, Dad, I've been talking to a friend of mine who is taking voice lessons at the Conservatory of Music where they also teach drama. I thought I might go there."

"Check it out" he replied.

I promptly found a better option — a brand new Theater School, established by the Jewish Community Center's Resident Theater on Linwood Boulevard. It wasn't too expensive and my father told me to go ahead.

Theater School was an exciting place and I learned a lot. The classrooms, instead of having row on row of desks, were stages and back stages and we sat on sofas and chairs. The first year was exhilarating and I felt I had found my place.

While there, I performed in a WPA version of radio called "Footlights of the Air" on WDAF. It was produced, directed and narrated by Brad Crandall Sr., a professional actor, who had a voice like a pipe organ. This presentation was an offshoot of the Works Progress Administration, a New Deal government program where out-of-work actors and others were paid for performing. I didn't receive any money; I was only looking for experience.

One assignment was to correct the performance of the new sound-effects person, who was making the wrong sounds at the wrong time.

"You can't make a lot of inappropriate noise," I advised her, "You're over here moving things around and banging them and making every kind of noise except the kind we want."

I hadn't taken into account that in the upcoming scene, one of the actors was to become angry and say, "I'm leaving this place once and for all."   At that point the sound-effects person was supposed to slam the door.   Remembering what I had told her, she opened the door gently so as to make barely a sound and then closed it just as gently.   Brad Crandall looked at me with little forgiveness in his eyes.

"Footlights of the Air" lasted only one more season.   As for Theater School, just as I was about to recommend to my father that I continue a second year, the school abruptly closed.   Herbert Drake, our great instructor, announced to the class that he was leaving.   He had been thinking it over and after having spent a lifetime in the theater, part of it as a director in New York, he had decided that he would rather raise apples than actors. He was going to start an apple farm in eastern Kansas.

Now what? There wasn't a job for an actor anywhere in Kansas City And I didn't want to go anywhere else. I knew right from the start I was married to this town.

Shortly after theater school ended, I was seated in a booth in my Dad's drugstore with friends and one of them hit upon something.

"You have a trained voice," he said. "Why don't you go into radio?"

Indeed, there were all those times I had fantasized about being a radio announcer. Maybe that's what I could do with my one-year education in theater.

That was in 1939. For the next year I made the rounds of program managers, hoping that they would remember me. I got

43

to know radio announcers, hoping that they would tip me off when a job came open. Although I made a lot of contacts, after a year I was still not employed. I bided my time working as a clerk and sometimes at the soda fountain in my father's drugstore, hoping and praying that I could someday escape all that. Meanwhile, I began to think like a radio man.

Out of our drugstore at Linwood and Troost we also operated a bus station and I was in charge of calling the buses. That gave me the chance to get hold of a microphone. I'd take the evening newspapers, *The Journal-Post* and *The Kansas City Star*, duck behind the counter and do a newscast over the public address system for the customers.

"And now, here is the evening news…," I began, reading the headlines and then the main stories. As far as the customers in the drugstore knew, the voice was coming from a radio. Later, I found out, Jim Lehrer got his start calling buses in Victoria, Texas, at the same time I was calling buses in Kansas City. We both worked with the same outfit, Crown Coach Lines, and we both thought we did a good job. But time was short to make the announcements, so we had to talk fast. More often than not, our words came out garbled and the passengers wound up having to figure out what we had just said.

The first time I heard my own voice played back to me on a wire recorder, I couldn't believe it. I had worked so hard to try to prepare myself — had even gone to theater school to develop my voice — but just listen! This high, nasal voice is a result of all that effort?

I would have been ready to give up — except that the alternative was a life spent at the drugstore, making sodas, selling bus tickets, and contemplating the ultimate use of condoms kept near the cash register. Using everything short of self-hypnosis, I kept myself focused on a radio career. At one point, I got a small break. Briefly at KMBC radio I acted out a series about great hymns and how they came to be written. KMBC was owned by the RLDS church at that time and my mother was a member of the church. She suggested that I audition for the job and I got it, but it lasted only about a year. During that year I was green with envy for a KMBC staffer who had a deep, beautiful radio voice — unfortunately, I was never quite sure of his name.

During those tough times for me, a neighbor named Guy Runnion took me under his wing. Guy and I lived in the same block, but there was a world of difference between us. While I pined for the most humble job in broadcasting, Guy had the top news spot in town — night announcer and newsman at WDAF radio. I was much younger and much smaller than Guy, yet he was kind enough to teach me things. I remember one of his lectures well:

"Listen, little chum, you have to learn to speak with authority. You must protect this at all times. Let's say you are doing a long story and right near the start you realize that you have mispronounced a word. You know the word, but for some reason you mispronounced it. This is where the test comes. Even if this word appears seven more times in the story, you must repeat it in the same erroneous fashion. Don't worry about it, because if you truly speak with authority, your public will accept it.   A great many of them will believe that they had the pronunciation wrong, or it has changed.   That's what happens, boy, when you speak with authority. If you falter, all is lost."

Guy Runnion gave me some writing work on a soap-opera comedy series that he wanted to produce called "The Bim and the Bloke." The show, however, didn't get off the ground. Even after writing several episodes, I wasn't sure what a "bim" was. Later, I found out that Guy was referring to a "bimbo," slang for a thickheaded woman.   The bloke was her male friend. When all was said and done, I was as unemployed in radio as ever.

One day in 1940 a break came. I got a call from a friend, Harry Becker, a man who had spent his career working for small, usually low-power radio stations — what we in the trade called "peanut whistles." There was an opening, he told me, at KDRO in Sedalia, Missouri. I got an interview there and was hired on the spot. During my first shift, I looked over the log. There were several hillbilly singers who played for an hour, some newscasts and — winding up my day at 5 p.m. — a sports report.

I am less of a sports fan than anyone who ever lived, and that turned out to be a major obstacle. Night after night, as the baseball reports came over the wire-service teletype, I struggled to cut them up and deliver them by reading one story after another. It didn't occur to me to arrange the teams by league; I had no idea which team was in the American League and which in the National. My pronunciation of the ballplayers' names was worse, even ones as famous as Joe DiMaggio. Each day after the sports segment, one of the station owners read me a list of my errors, correcting the pronunciation of names and explaining which teams were in which league. The more I listened, the more confused I became.

By Friday of my first week I was in the middle of the 5 o'clock sports when I glanced through the glass window of the studio and saw the giant head of one of the station owners, his face red. When I emerged from the studio, he asked me, "Do you think you will ever learn the difference between the American League and the National League?"

I replied, speaking honestly, "I'm afraid I might not." He responded just as honestly that my career with KDRO was over, and handed me my check. That night I rode back to Kansas City with a friend. As we drove along Highway 50, I looked out into the night and thought about all the time I'd spent calling all those stations, finally finding a job and losing it after only a week. I got over it by remembering what I had really lost — a job that paid a measly $12.50 a week.

News always flies between radio stations and within a day or so I received another phone call from Harry Becker, who heard that I had parted company with Sedalia. Would I be interested in joining him at KVAK in Atchison, Kansas? The pay, he said, was $15 a week and there were no sportscasts to do. I snapped up the opportunity. Harry was the program director at KVAK, but he was sick and tired of it. He had arranged with the owners for me to take over as program director as soon as I knew the ropes. In

Harry's voice was a sly "gotcha" sound.

"Very well," I said, "and upon my ascension to the throne, I'm assigning you to work the morning sign-on shift."

What I didn't know was that the management at KVAK had previous experience with Harry on early-morning assignments. Harry liked to stay up late, so at 7 a.m. it was difficult for him to remain awake to do a full-length newscast. One of my duties, then, was to arise at 7 o'clock each morning in my room across the street at the Atchison Hotel, turn on my radio and listen to Harry for the duration of the news to make sure he didn't go to sleep. I thought this would be unlikely. About four days into the job I woke up and turned on the radio. Everything seemed to be going well, but then I heard Harry say, "And in Great Britain today as the crisis worsens... Prime Minister... Winston... zzzzzzz...."

I jumped out of bed, put on a robe and slippers, took the elevator downstairs, ran through the lobby, and crossed the street. I raced through the entrance, up one long flight of noisy stairs, and through three sets of doors. There in the studio I saw Harry slumped forward. I gave him a quick punch on the left shoulder.

"...Churchill," he said into the microphone, and resumed where he had left off.

There were some hardships in Atchison for a man who was young and single. I spent a good deal of time at the drugstore across the street from the radio station and was enamored with a lady who worked behind the soda fountain. One day I screwed up my courage and asked, "Would you like to go out sometime?" Her reply: "Oh, no. No parent in town would let their daughter go out with one of the radio guys." A couple of staffers at the radio station, I discovered later, had left a few local girls in a family way. The staffers were fired, but that was little help to me.

At the station we strongly believed that much of the time nobody was listening. Sometimes we'd throw open the telephone line and ask listeners to call in with a request for music. We'd wait and wait, yet no calls came.

Commercials were few, and the copy wasn't changed too often on those we had. One in particular was a tongue-twister for all of us: "The Norge Royal Rolater Refrigerator." The product was mentioned two or three times in the script, and the commercial stayed on our logs a maddeningly long time. In those days ad agencies knew little if anything about focus groups or test markets. They focused on repetition.

Harry Becker went back on the evening shift, where one night he was to read romantic poetry from one or two dog-eared books over soft, recorded organ music. Just before beginning, he recognized the signs of an oncoming attack of intestinal flu. He couldn't endure staying in the studio for 30 minutes, so he wired the console to what we called the "throne room." As 11 o'clock rolled around, Harry began reading poems one after another, seated upon the "throne." It was a perfect solution, except that in the last minute of the show he forgot where he was and flushed. No one called to complain, and for once we were glad that not many people were listening.

Every now and then in the middle of a thunderstorm the

chief engineer called in to tell us that we were off the air because
the tower had been hit by lightning. On one of the worst nights he
called to say: "You'll be off for quite a while. Lightning just blew
me clear out of the transmitter shack."

KVAK had an auxiliary studio in the city of Leavenworth,
and I worked there from time to time. In a typical shift, I'd
introduce preachers trying to attract new members for their
churches. Some preached and others sang, but either way we
collected the money in advance. I thought that was unique to our
station, but I later read a book by Steve Allen, who spent his early
career working in small radio stations. Cash in advance was the
rule, Allen said, and preachers had to be watched more closely than
politicians.

Once a week we'd have a show with someone representing
one of the veterans groups. One day our speaker was a
distinguished war hero. He was a nice guy, and we had a little chat
before we went on. I explained that we had a single stand-up
microphone. I would introduce him and then step aside so he
could deliver his speech. As I was saying the final words of the
introduction, I heard a heavy thud. He had fainted. War hero that
he was, he was not up to facing a microphone that day.   Several
people came to his aid, and I turned back to the microphone and
said: "We're sorry. The program originally scheduled for this time
will not be heard." I then rushed to put on a record.

One day I was assigned to Leavenworth to describe a
patriotic parade. At 1 p.m. they cued me, and I put on my

microphone and began to talk. There wasn't much of a crowd.

"So far, it doesn't appear that there are many people out," I reported, "but it's a little chilly and a lot of people are probably inside the store shopping. When they hear the bands playing they'll come out. They'll be coming around the bend up the street. We have a good vantage point as they will be coming right by the drugstore."

I continued to talk about the upcoming parade — in our business we call it "vamping" — and about the weather and about the drums I thought I heard in the distance.

"I think the parade is starting a little late," I reported, "but here they come."

Still no one came out of the stores to watch. There was only one man, leaning on a pole, who paid any attention at all to what I was saying.

"Good afternoon, sir," I said to him. "I bet you came downtown to see the big parade."

He paused and in a dry voice said, "The parade was yesterday."

That left me with a big chunk of an hour to fill. Back in Atchison, everybody had probably left the station and trooped down to Montezuma's, a congenial place with large steins of beer and some pretty good chili. You can bet there was a scramble to get back to the station and get back on the air.

I can still hear that old guy saying, "The parade was yesterday."

At KVAK we weren't paid much, but we had fun. There were

few commercials to read and management paid us little attention. To break the monotony, we tried various antics. On the Fourth of July someone might position a large firecracker across the table from the newscaster who was delivering the news, just far enough to be out of his reach. One day, I was that man. The tricksters placed the firecracker outside my reach. Smiling fiendishly, they lit the fuse and with a ceremonial sweep walked away. I watched the fuse go down and tried to stay on the air until the last. Finally I said on the air, "I will return in a moment," and ducked beneath the table. I waited and waited and finally heard "fs-s-s-s-ss" and the firecracker fizzled out. I got out from under the table and said, "Also in the news today...."

I had a life-changing experience while working at KVAK. One cold winter morning when it was about five degrees above zero, I was walking across the street on my way to work, quite full of myself. Being a radio announcer, I believed, was hot stuff. At a traffic light I noticed an old man digging a hole in the street for one of the utilities, and his face was red from the cold. He looked up at me and said, "Well boy, what do you do for a living?" Proudly I responded, "I am a radio announcer." Instead of being struck with the glory of it, his response was: "Well, don't screw it up, boy. That's nice indoor work." It's been more than a half a century, but I can still see that man, red from the cold, and I can still hear his words. Chastened, I went on to work.

One of the hazards in a small station was the equipment, much of which was decrepit. Things like "on" and "off" switches

Mary Gilmore and Walton Martin Bodine —
my parents' wedding portrait.

Walton Marshall Bodine. My infant
portrait, made in the early 1920s.

With Mom

Above: Suits me! Coat, vest and my first long pants.

Right: Snapshots from a photo booth, Union Station.

Inside Bodine's All Night Drug Store at Troost Avenue and Linwood Boulevard. Soda fountain is at the far end.

Special Collections, Kansas City Public Library, Kansas City, Missouri

Above: Hub of the neighborhood. Looking west on Linwood at Troost just after Christmas, 1928. Bodine's is on the southwest corner, left.

Left: Portrait of the author as a young man.

Our wedding day: Bernadine and me in 1950.

A Bodine family portrait.

Bernie and me in the late 1980s.

could not be relied on. Once, an announcer came to the end of a long commercial for a clothing store, slammed the switch off and watched the "On the Air" light go out. Then he said, "That's a bunch of crap if I ever heard it." But the microphone had remained on. Coincidentally, the light had burned out at just that moment. His evaluation of the commercial went blaring over the air. Once again, we never heard from anyone — not even the sponsor.

Listeners or no, we always needed announcers, and Harry and I called Grayson Enlow, a mutual friend with a great voice who accepted our offer. Grayson was a giant of a man who had to lower his head a little to come through the doorway. He could fill it from side to side, too. Grayson had a natural dignity and an imposing presence. I told him he would make a great president of the United States if only he knew anything about it. Grayson did better than any of us. He went on to New York City where he worked for the Mutual Broadcasting System. He announced opera concerts on Mutual, played various roles on the network's programs, and did a brief stint in 1951 as Lamont Cranston in "The Shadow." You could hear him saying, "Who knows what evil lurks in the hearts of men? The Shadow knows."

Another man who worked at KVAK also performed as a clown at Memorial Hall in Atchison. Frank Wiziarde went on to become known to generations of Kansas City children as Whizzo the Clown.

I'll never forget my last encounter with Frank in Kansas City years after. I entered the backstage area as he was performing. There was Frank, whirling around, singing and dancing and making the kids laugh. When the music came to an end, he whirled offstage toward us. Putting his hand into his pocket, he pulled out a cigarette before he had even stopped turning and his face changed from happy clown to sober with sad eyes. He looked up and said, "Hi, ya, Wally." As we chatted he said that times were tough at home; a family member had serious health problems. Just then, the music started again. He heard his cue, dropped the cigarette, put on the smile and went whirling back on stage where the kids shouted "Whizzo! Whizzo!" It wasn't long afterward that Whizzo died of cancer. Whizzo didn't expect a lot of attention, but when he died a lot of people took notice — those who had enjoyed his work and those who had used his television appearances as a babysitter for their kids. The demise of Whizzo was front-page news in *The Kansas City Star*.

The one year-plus that I spent in Atchison gave me a chance to try some of the advice of my mentor, Guy Runnion. In news copy, he had told me, if you're sight-reading try to read ahead a line or so. He recalled the time when he was reading some news and looked ahead, seeing a preposterously long name. It turned out to be the first name of the wife of Joseph Stalin. She had just died. Instead of trying to pronounce the name, he simply said, "The wife of the Soviet dictator, Joseph Stalin, died today. Mrs. Stalin married her husband in 1919."

Then there's the matter of pronunciations in general. You suddenly realize that you've mispronounced a word. What do you do, particularly when the word reappears? Guy's advice was to decide how to say it and then say it with authority. I used his advice

54

one day while I was program director at KVAK. We had various people who tried to do women's shows. For the most part these consisted of reading news releases from General Mills, Pillsbury and others about dishes that could be prepared with their products.

One of the ladies who read the recipes over the air had a habit of not showing up now and then, so one day I was called on to take her place. I grabbed a handful of news releases, sat down and started to read a recipe. There were a lot of words I had never seen before. One came up as I began to read the recipe for lemon meringue pie. Boldly, I pronounced it "MARE-en-gew." It occurred about three more times, and I stuck with the mispronunciation, saying it with authority, "Lemon MARE-en-gew pie." It must have been all right with most of the listeners because there was only one call.

"Are you that fool that was just on the air trying to say lemon *meringue* pie?" the woman asked.

"Yes, I am."

"Well, I hope you learned something."

My fondest hope was that the others who heard me mispronounce it four times thought that it must be the dictionary's second choice.

My most unforgettable experience in Atchison came on December 8, 1941, the day after the Japanese attack on Pearl Harbor. Because Atchison girls wouldn't associate with radio guys, I usually went home to Kansas City on weekends to improve my social life.

As I returned by train to Atchison that Monday, I was concerned about how we would cover the war. KVAK was a tiny station with no network and a terrible wire service, far below the standards of the United Press and Associated Press. We would stand around, looking at our wire service teletype as it slowly clanked out stories and shout at it as if to tell the operator on the other end to hurry up.

As program director, I knew if all we did was play music on the day after Pearl Harbor, our audience would plummet to zero.

Then, inspiration struck: I'd go down to the street, my colleagues would get a mike with a long cord and drop it through the window to me, and I would interview people. We'd see what Mr. and Mrs. Atchison had to say about the dreadful event. So I went downstairs prepared for a chilly morning and watched the microphone slowly descending into my hands.

Reality quickly set in. Mr. and Mrs. Atchison weren't out on the street. They were home or in stores listening to the radio — probably other stations. I was out there alone. I began to ad lib and then suddenly an elderly lady came around the corner. She had neat gray hair, wore a dark dress and had a cameo around her neck.

"KVAK is interviewing the people of Atchison," I said to her. "We want to know what you think about the Japanese attack on Pearl Harbor."

"Oh, yes," she said, "I've got two nephews that I just love and they're both out there in the Philippines and if those goddamn sons of bitches lay a hand on those boys…."

I felt a tug and the microphone left my hand, rose slowly up the side of the building and through the studio window. The lady kept talking, directing her tirade at my empty hand. When she finished I thanked her.

Shortly after Pearl Harbor we had what we thought was a great patriotic idea. We decided to hold a contest asking listeners to finish the sentence, "We should all buy war bonds because…." The prizes were big boxes of Bit-O-Honey Candy bars. As usual, we got no response, and were stuck with a large supply of candy. I called a girlfriend at St. Mary College near Leavenworth and said, "Harriet, if you would like to get some wonderful candy bars for everybody on your floor there, all you have to do is have everyone fill out an entry finishing the sentence, `We should all buy war bonds because….' "

Every entry, of course, was a winner and we dispatched almost all of the boxes of candy bars. The last box went to an honest-to-goodness entrant, proving we had at least one listener out there. At one point, Harriet called and said they were overwhelmed and would like to send some back. No, I told her, that would be unpatriotic.

These days, KVAK has been replaced by a far more modern radio station. I was interviewed on it in recent years, and throughout the program I could hear a pipe organ. At a station break, I was told that the tenant next door was a funeral home. Whenever there was a funeral, the organ could be heard through the wall. Our interview continued, accompanied by music meant for some departed soul. That took me back to the KVAK of my day, when the station was right over the Latenser Music Company. I could always tell when a piano demonstration was going on downstairs because in the middle of my 9 p.m. newscast I'd hear the same melody over and over. You could tell the good piano players from the bad even if you were concentrating on the news.

In Sedalia, Atchison and Leavenworth, the pay was never more than $15 a week. We'd hear fabulous stories about announcers at KMBC in Kansas City with great voices and great paychecks — as much as $35 a week. I aimed to work my way back to the city and up to one of those jobs, and got the ball rolling in 1941 when an old friend working at KCKN in Kansas City, Kansas, told me about a job opening there.

———————————

KCKN was catching on by playing popular music all day. Getting hired was remarkably easy — perhaps because of the wartime turnover. One by one, as the country mobilized for World War II, staff members disappeared into one branch of the armed services or another. Before too many months had passed, I was caught up in the exodus, too.

The U.S. Maritime Service, which trained men for the Merchant Marine, was looking for people with broadcast experience. We were to travel to various places and try to persuade veteran seafarers — particularly captains and engineers — to join the Merchant Marine. So I was sworn in to the Naval Reserve, Class M1, the U.S. Maritime Service. My job was to appear on radio, stir up interest in the U.S. Merchant Marine, and run recruiting offices. While stationed at Hoffman Island in New York Harbor, I managed to rank second in a large class of the administrative personnel school. The man in third place was a lieutenant commander. That was some comfort, but then I was shipped out to a post at Port Arthur, Texas, a tough seaport town.

On my first night in Port Arthur I went out for a stroll. As I passed a bar a beer bottle came flying out, just past my nose. I thought about looking to see who threw it, but it seemed wiser to keep on walking.

At the end of the war in 1945 I returned to KCKN, and went to work alongside C. Edward Clark, a one-time bellhop who later was designated by WHB "The Morning Mayor of 12th Street." We handled two shows that were popular in their day.

One was "Katz Dance with America" in the early evening. With more than one announcer and sound effects, the radio audience was led to believe that it was hearing from top bands performing in cities across the country. One of us might say, "And now to Philadelphia for the sounds of...." and play a record by that band. Of course, everything was taking place in the studio of KCKN. The other show was "Helzberg's Romance in Rhythm," airing in the afternoon. Romantic music was played for one hour to try to get people to come into the store to buy engagement rings. Eddie Clark had a deep, imposing voice and when he announced the show — "Romance in Rhythm, brought to you by Helzberg's, home of Certified Perfect diamonds" — he probably scored many a sale for Helzberg's. Clark rose in the business and he later moved to Cleveland radio, where he picked up the title "Morning Mayor of Cleveland."

KCKN broke from its popular music format when Senator Robert A. Taft visited Kansas City to promote the Taft-Hartley labor bill, of which he was co-author. KCKN was chosen to be the originating station for Taft's half-hour speech to the nation, which made station executives all atwitter. That joy did not extend to the announcing staff. We were solidly union and opposed to the Taft-Hartley bill, which restricted various union activities. The senator asked that the program director, George Stump, sit across the room from him with time cues written on large cards. Stump was to pull the cards away and drop them so that the new time cue would come in sight. Before they began, Stump and Taft left the room for a while and some imp on the staff stuck in another card that said "Oh, shut your big mouth." The speech got under way, and went along smoothly, Stump removing the cards one by one, until near the end. As Taft looked down at his speech copy, George removed what he thought was the next to the last card. To his dismay there was the one that said, "Oh, shut your big mouth." He almost fainted, but he managed to pull it away just before the senator looked back up.

Not long after, I got the chance to leave the life of record-playing when WDAF radio's program director, Harry Kaufmann, called me for an audition. Harry's method of auditioning was to have a job candidate read the afternoon paper to him. He was almost blind, so that was a way for him to find out what was going on in the world while he evaluated new talent for the radio. My reading passed and in 1946 I began my career with WDAF. It was to last almost two decades.

INTERLUDE

Why Sports and I Don't Get Along

Life can be difficult if you are not by nature a sportsman. I'm a perfect example. Here I am, a small island of indifference surrounded by a sea of sports hype. I'm sure there are others out there like me — people for whom the opening day of baseball is just one more day. Whether it's baseball, basketball, or football, as one who is sports-immune it was no wonder I was fired from my first job in radio, announcing sports at KDRO in Sedalia.

As a child, I played a lot of those games in the back yard of 712 Linwood where I lived. But later in life, watching them was a yawner for me. As a student at Westport High School, I seldom attended football games.

But after I went to work at KVAK in Atchison, there was a day I couldn't escape an encounter with pigskins and players. One cold Thanksgiving we were covering a football game between Atchison and Leavenworth. My job was to sit with the play-by-play announcer. Management promised me I wouldn't have to comment on the game. All I had to do was read a commercial for a restaurant. The platform where we perched was raised precariously above everything else, unprotected from the chill wind. With each gust, our primitive press box responded with a shudder. I kept wondering whether the commercial-reader — me — and play-by-play man would be wiped out mid-game.

*　　　*　　　*

On one other occasion I was pressed into service in sports when KCKN asked me to be the color announcer for a hockey game. Although I protested that I'd never even seen a hockey game, they insisted. It turned out this was no ordinary broadcast, but one we were originating for a network of four or five stations. I knew I was sure to disgrace myself on one station. Now it turned out I'd be doing that on several at the same time. Frenetic, I went to see Larry Ray, the play-by-play announcer and a happy, smiling man for whom sports was one of the great joys of life. "It'll be all right," he said, his eyes twinkling. "All you have to do is fill 15 minutes between periods. That won't be hard."

"*Fifteen minutes!*"

My fate was sealed and I reported to the Pla-

Mor hockey rink just off Main Street, where Larry and I settled down in the spot reserved for the play-by-play man and for the announcer who filled the time when the former was gone. I sat through the first part of the game, watching and trying to understand it. Mostly I felt a strong sense of dread. Every moment brought me closer to the time when Larry Ray would say, "I'll be back in a few minutes, but in the meantime here is Walt Bodine...."

When that moment arrived I began to jabber, meanwhile turning sidewise to watch Larry going up the stairs, ever higher in the arena, and ever closer to the hot dogs and drinks. Turning back to the microphone, I figured I had filled all of 10 seconds. Now, what to do for the rest? Right then, a little vehicle appeared on the ice, driven by a man who knew how to manipulate it up and down and back and forth to smooth the surface. I confided my thoughts to the listeners, thoughts such as "I'll bet that guy gets cold."

After a while, I resorted to theft. Across the aisle from where I sat, someone had gone to the refreshment stand and left behind a program. I grabbed it, thumbed quickly through and found a page describing the penalty box. There was my salvation. I made it last, reading line by line and giving commentary along the way. I even tried injecting humor, but how funny can you be when you feel as if you're headed for the guillotine? My watch showed that only four minutes had gone by. I'm sure there were people who gave up hockey forever that night, overdosed on data about the penalty box. Eventually I began to describe the fans as they returned to their seats, the women wearing festive colors and the men wearing sports-fan getup. When it was over, I was literally so full of perspiration it was as if I had fallen into a pool.

Larry Ray returned, slid back into his seat and flashed me that big smile. A sense of relief came over me; however horrible it was, it was over. When I went to the office the next day, no one said a thing to me about it. Again I was brought face to face with the phenomenon that radio managers and owners seldom, if ever, listen to their own stations at night.

CHAPTER IV

Paying My Dues at WDAF - Farm News, Soap Operas, Poetry Readings - And Now the News - Perils of Live TV - Bobby Greenlease - My Own Weather Disaster - Fiery Death on Southwest Boulevard - Khrushchev in the Cornfield

By the end of the war, radio was changing. For one thing, announcers gradually abandoned pomposity. In the early years of the medium, some announcers wore tuxedos — as if to make their delivery more professional. Then they figured out that they didn't have to wear a tuxedo, but simply to say they had one on, and the radio audience would never know the difference. Eventually broadcasters realized that audiences preferred announcers who sounded down to earth. To score valued ratings points, some announcers even verged on chatty. Today the stuffed-shirt model has been discarded, and most announcers have a warm, friendly on-air personality. To some it comes naturally. Others have to work themselves up to it.

At the beginning of my tenure with WDAF radio in 1946 I was assigned to an early-morning shift with Al Christy, who later became an actor in dinner theater and in a few movies, such as *In Cold Blood*, *When Harry Met Sally* and *Mr. and Mrs. Bridge*. The theme music of our program was "Syncopated Swing," but that was about as swinging as it got. For the most part, our show was aimed at a farm audience. I wondered about all the city dwellers at their breakfast tables, ready to take a big bite of sausage, when I'd come on with this line: "Friends, are your hogs diseased?" Another commercial suggested Dannen Pig Slopper: "It will give you many more pounds of rich, ropey slop." Imagine trying that on a drive-time crowd today!

One of the most tedious passages of my broadcasting career was a mid-day shift at WDAF when I had to listen to almost 20 soap operas from NBC, one after another. Soaps lasted 15 minutes each, and they were not great works of literature. They were the likes of "Young Widder Brown," "Mary Noble, Backstage Wife," "Stella Dallas" — and I'll spare you the rest.

The soaps were encumbered with a multitude of commercials, opening with what we called a cowcatcher, a brief commercial of one or two lines. Then came the theme music, and the announcement of the title, and then a full-length commercial. Finally, the story picked up where it had left off the day before, only to stop again about 12 1/2 minutes later for one more full commercial and then a small commercial. Except for jumping every 15 minutes to announce the time and the station identification, my job was to monitor program after program, and to log which commercials went on and exactly how long they lasted. It took patience to do that day after day.

A host of actors in Chicago and New York filled the roles, and their voices became familiar. The writing left much to be desired. "Just Plain Bill, Barber of Hartville," was announced as "the story of a man who might be living right next door to you — the real-life story of people just like people we all know." One day when Bill was kidnapped by a gang of jewel thieves, it occurred to me that his day-to-day life was not like that of any of his listeners. Improbable as they were, these stories had a loyal following.

For soap-opera actors, the biggest worry was to receive a script for the next day's show and read that their character was scheduled to die. Dying on the air meant unemployment in real life. On the appointed day, when their character was about to kick the bucket, the affected actors' voices were full of emotion.

I had something of the same experience with a national children's show produced in Kansas City called "The Air Adventures of Jimmy Allen." It was about a kid named Jimmy and his older partner named Speed. Speed was Shelby Storck, a newscaster who later went into television production and public relations, and Jimmy was John Schlicter, a former disc jockey and later insurance executive. I played Mr. Jenkins, manager of the small airport where the boys took off and landed. I would begin a series of episodes by calling the boys in my office to tell them something like this: "There is a group of bank robbers operating in the Latin American countries, hitting one bank after another. Boys, I want you to go down there and help find those rascals and see that they are turned over to local police." That would be the end of my work on the show until the entire adventure was over, which could take several weeks. Then I would be called back in and, as Mr. Jenkins, say, "Fellows, that was a brave mission, and you carried it out wonderfully, but now I have an even greater

67

challenge for you." I'd unveil their next assignment and languish still more weeks until Mr. Jenkins was to re-appear.

All this was before the days of tape recording. Recording was done on big, black discs and there was no such thing as editing out mistakes. When we recorded an episode, the last few minutes were tense because one slip of the tongue or an inadvertent noise meant starting over. One day, in the final minutes of recording, several fire engines rolled past the building and their sound went right on to the record. When that happened you could almost cry as you picked up the script to start over.

Until time and changing audience tastes brought them to an end, poetry shows were a regular feature on radio. I made many appearances on WDAF radio's venerable late-night program, "Moonbeams." It came on after 11 p.m. with a live studio orchestra playing, "Moonbeams shining soft above, shine upon the one I love...." This was fancy stuff. Background for other stations' poetry readings was a single pipe organ or a recording, but WDAF had a live orchestra. The difficulty was that the orchestra was in Studio A and the announcer in Studio B. Never did the announcer and the conductor consult in advance, and the orchestra couldn't hear the announcer. Once the music started the announcer quickly had to find a poem to fit the mood. Usually this arrangement worked. Sometimes it didn't. One Halloween night, I was reading Edgar Allen Poe's "The Raven," and the orchestra began with a somber selection. When I was only about halfway through the poem, the orchestra switched to the sprightlier "Minuet in G." All I could do was finish as quickly as possible and look for another verse.

My old mentor, Guy Runnion, gave me advice about poetry shows like these, ones where there was no plan and your only tools were a few ragged poetry books. Approaching the end of the show, you could find yourself faced with filling a short time. Guy recommended keeping a supply of short verses for those occasions. This was one:

"I'm glad the sky above is blue;
I'm glad the grass is green,
With lots and lots of nice, fresh air
All sandwiched in between"

These I came to call "nothing" verses. I wrote a few of my own:

"The fortune-teller sits in a little room
Where the lights are very dim.
He stares into his crystal ball
And it stares back at him."

"Of all the nothing poems
Be they north, south, east or west,
You must admit that this one
Ranks with the very best."

On Thursday nights WDAF broadcast a show with live

music sponsored by D.W. Newcomer's Sons funeral home — a live show selling death, you might say. I was there to get the sponsor's point across, but while delivering a commercial about D.W. Newcomer's crematory and columbarium I added gestures that broke up the lead violinist, Karl. He shook with barely stifled laughter, which fortunately was overridden by his music.

Eventually, I escaped these strange shows and began doing the nightly news at 5:45 and 10 p.m. In the postwar years when I started working there, WDAF radio was on the third floor of *The Kansas City Star* building at 18th Street and Grand Avenue. I gathered my material in *The Star's* second-floor newsroom, where there were rows of yellow, wooden desks, each with a large spittoon beside it. They reflected the days when reporters chewed lots of tobacco and putting out a daily newspaper required a great deal of spitting. The spittoons were cleaned and shined by a group of employees who wore blue over-alls. These Blue Men arrived about mid-evening to do their chores. Those of us who were younger puzzled at the importance attached to the spittoons; we hardly knew what to do with them.

Winifred Shields, a reporter and later art critic, was well dressed and elegant. I used to watch Winnie, whose desk was just across from mine, as she entered the newsroom and took a wide detour to avoid contact with the spittoons. Winnie wasn't a fussbudget, just a neat and beautiful person. A cuspidor simply wasn't going to be part of her world.

In the center of the newsroom sat a bank of telephones, separated from one another by little panes of glass. When young Tom Leathers was breaking in, he was assigned to write obituaries. Early in the evening the phones would ring and a copyboy would shout across the room, "Mr. Leathers, on four." As the evening wore on and the honchos whose desks lined the south wall left, the copyboy would shout, "Mr. Leathers, death on seven." I used to kid Leathers that out there somewhere was a black-robed figure calling from a telephone booth saying, "OK, Tom, I got another one."

The newsroom was much more fun later in the evening. During the day there were too many office climbers trying to get close to the boss. One in particular rushed each day to help Roy Roberts, the president of *The Star*, on with his coat at lunch time and again at quitting time.

Yet there was an array of interesting people, too, in *The Star* newsroom. Reg Tolley was one of them, memorable mainly because he sat across from me. He was a great reporter with a sense of humor, and I was in awe of him. He covered City Hall for many years, and he kept pocketfuls of notes about loading zones approved here and tax increases turned down there. After spending a long day with the denizens of City Hall, Reg came in and said little until he started writing. Then he began to loosen up and made for great company.

The police radio was good for excitement. It led me to the scene of my first murder case, at 39th and Main streets. A cab driver had shot another cab driver who'd been fooling around with his wife. As I made out the shape of a body under a brown police blanket, a thought haunted me: how quickly life could be taken away. The victim had been among the living only 15 minutes before.

On some of these excursions I experienced a few quirky policemen. One night the jazz pianist and singer Julia Lee was playing at a joint at Linwood and Main, and there was a tiny Austin automobile parked illegally on a grassy strip nearby. A big, overweight cop wearing shell-rimmed glasses arrived on the scene and, as a crowd gathered around, tried to figure out what to do. He must have been having difficulties with his superiors, because he turned to the onlookers and delivered a short speech.

"Whatever I do here," he said, "I'm going to be wrong. I could get two or three of you to help me pick this car up and carry it right over there by the curb and put it down and it would be legally parked. We could all go in peace. But someone at headquarters might think that constituted an act of theft.

"I could just leave it where it is right now and maybe get a witness or two. But someone would say that the officer didn't handle this right. He should have had this car towed in to the police garage."

The folks standing around were inclined to say: "Yes, you're telling them. That's right, officer." He left the car just as it was, but with a ticket on it for illegal parking. He stepped back in his patrol car and rode off, contented that he made a Solomon-like decision and avoided being cited by the folks down at headquarters.

At WDAF radio, I had my first experience as a weatherman. The station offered me extra money to take on the job, and so I had to get up each morning and come to work about 7:30 a.m., when I would chat on the phone with some grouchy folks at the local Weather Bureau to get a Kansas City forecast. At 10 minutes after

8, right after the news, I would come on and attempt to make the weather interesting, even though I was usually bored by it. To add interest, I'd spin out little weather rhymes each day, along with reading a commercial from the Santa Fe railroad. The rhymes were terrible. One example:

"If wet weather gives you a pain, look out friend:
There is going to be rain."

Contrast all that with the modern television weather forecaster who sits in what looks like a science laboratory — almost like the set of the old "Frankenstein" movie — with gauges and gadgets and blinking lights and radar.

I was on hand for the beginning of the miracle of television in Kansas City. The first station was WDAF-TV, owned by *The Star*. When it began broadcasting in 1949, WDAF showed only a test pattern — the head of an Indian in full headdress. The relative few who owned television sets within reach of the signal would actually sit and look at the test pattern just because it had come to them through the air. I imagined some family out there in infant TV land; the husband calls to his wife: "Martha, come in here. That thing just moved!"

In my early days of television I watched the antics of Kansas City's first anchorman, Randall Jessee. Not only was he WDAF's primary newscaster, but also the announcer of choice for all kinds of commercial products and special events. Randall was popular and it was easy to see why. He was a husky guy with dark, curly hair and mischievous blue eyes, and you could tell he didn't mind having a little nip with a friend at the bar. In the early 1950s, more Kansas Citians knew who Randall Jessee was than knew who was governor of Missouri.

There was no such thing as videotape then. Everything that wasn't on film was live. Macy's, a big advertiser, was advertising a real novelty — furniture made of a strong and pressure-resistant form of cardboard. Randall, a very big man, was there to show the audience that it was great stuff. He was to stand on the couch, jump once or twice and then give the price and announce where to buy it. When the time came, Randall stepped up on the couch, gave two little jumps, and the thing came crashing down. It looked, one of the directors later said, like the remains of a plane crash. Dust surrounded the wreckage, and sticking out of it was Randall's leg. That was the end of that commercial — and perhaps the product.

Once, Randall was involved in a large commercial production with two cameras. One camera was placed overhead, peering down on General Electric's new garbage disposal. Randall followed the script carefully all through the rehearsal. When it came time for the live performance, Randall began to talk about this wonderful new disposal. He took off the lid and the camera above lit up. Randall looked up at it and said, "I'm taking two agate marbles and I'm going to throw them in here." You could hear the noise as they dropped in. He put the lid back on.

"Now all you do is throw this switch," he said. When he threw it, there was a noise like World War III. He knew something was terribly wrong. But when you're on camera at the only TV station in town, you can't say, "Where's my mama?" or "Get me out of here." The script called for him to remove the lid once the machine had stopped whirring and show that the marbles had been ground to fine dust. Instead, the machine was a shambles. In the middle of it all sat the two marbles, which had survived in perfect shape.

Today a videotape crew would simply start over with a new take, but on that live broadcast the directors in the control booth did what the viewing public was doing — they looked on, astonished. It wasn't long before someone came up with a useful bit of advice for such situations: "Fade to black and think it over." Then the directors would go on to the next thing on the schedule and act as if nothing bad had happened.

There was a woman — let's call her Dorothea — who had a program for women in mid-morning and did a weekend children's show. When she was scheduled to interview Claire Booth Luce about her play "The Women," Dorothea thought about it and talked about it for days and rehearsed pronouncing the name. In the excitement of the actual interview, however, she managed to introduce Mrs. Luce as "Bare Loose Tooth."

On another occasion, we were having a spirited gathering of the staff in the announcer's booth, talking about an upcoming union contract. We kept an eye on the engineer, because we suspected him sometimes of tuning in on our meetings. In the middle of this Dorothea appeared in the control room and knocked vigorously on the glass window of the announcer's booth. We all turned around. She held up a picture that a child had sent of a robin. You could read her lips, saying, "Isn't that sweet?" Several of the staff members, already in a high state of emotion, turned and directed comments at her, none of them sweet. As we suspected, the engineer was listening in on our meeting so Dorothea heard it all. She took her bird picture and fled.

In 1953 the labor-management dispute boiled over, and we members of the American Federation of Television and Radio Artists voted to walk out over pay. Our strike was directed at *The Kansas City Star*, owner of WDAF radio and television. I was picked by union leadership to take charge of the picket line.

In a way, it was in my bloodlines to be an activist. Marshall, my middle name, was the last name of my maternal grandfather. In the 19th century, he worked in Kansas City's railroad yards stenciling numbers on freight cars. He was a devout socialist, so committed to the great socialist of his time, Eugene Debs, that his fellow workers called him "Debs." When my grandfather first came to Kansas City with his wife and kids he worked in the stockyards for $7 a week. I was no socialist, and I certainly made more than $7 a week, yet I took my new union assignment seriously.

My task was to ensure that pickets were out along Southwest Trafficway at rush hours. Many Kansas Citians were certain that *The Star*, mightiest of the media locally, could crush our action easily. The editorials denounced us, but quite a few people were on our side. As they sped by in their cars, they'd wave and honk their horns. Now and then, someone gave us the international sign of ill will. But mostly we got two fingers up in a "V" for victory.

As picket-line boss, I had a major crisis the first day. When I reported for duty about 8 a.m., there parked in front of the station were the automobiles owned by the people marching the line. Several of my co-workers were single and veterans of the business. They had saved their money and bought some nice cars. Lined up in full view were a Jaguar, a speedy-looking Oldsmobile and a Cadillac. I quickly gathered the picketers around me.

"We're underpaid and we're having a hard time," I said. "There are a lot of good-looking cars here, and it makes us look like a very rich picket line. Get 'em out of here."

They moved the stylish autos to Karnes Boulevard.

Each day of the strike, late in the afternoon, a woman pulled up in a limousine. She'd open the back door of the car and set up a little cocktail bar with some serious refreshments for our guys. What a strike!

We were front-page news at times, and once targets of a front-page editorial in *The Star's* morning edition, *The Times*. It blasted us because we wouldn't relent long enough for WDAF to carry the story of the crowning of Queen Elizabeth in Westminister Abbey. It made little difference in our public support. In the end, we won substantial raises.

When "The Tonight Show" with Steve Allen debuted in 1954, Randall Jessee and I hosted a local version called, "Tonight in Kansas City." We went on the air right before the network "Tonight." Randall did the news and sometimes a serious interview. Jay Barrington was the sportscaster, so embedded in his role that he'd call me "Coach" and Randall "Ace." I covered miscellaneous stories that were unusual or funny. Once I went downtown to see a car dealer who had a mynah bird that could talk a blue streak. While I was in the dealer's office the bird — clearly not enchanted with having visitors – spoke hardly at all. Nevertheless, we took the bird to the studio. At the scheduled time, I was to come on with the mynah bird so the viewers could hear him talk. Just before our time, the bird was talking away. The moment we went into the studio with its bright lights and busy stagehands, the mynah clammed up for three long minutes. Three minutes can be a very long time when you're on the air, live, talking to a bird that won't talk back. When my segment finally ended, the owner of the bird and I walked out of the studio. Promptly, the bird resumed its chatter. I looked at it and said, "Oh, shut up."

"The Today Show" originated in Kansas City in October 1955, when Dave Garroway was the host. One morning, "Today" broadcast from the American Royal and the next morning from Union Station. One night, Randall invited Garroway to dinner at his home in Coleman Highlands. As Garroway walked to the kitchen window he looked out at the moonlight playing on the waters of Randall's swimming pool and said, "You poor country sonofabitch—you have it tough, don't you?"

Later Randall was the master of ceremonies for an amateur hour at the Pla-Mor on Main Street. The sponsor of this show was the Jack Boring Stores, appliance dealers. The show was known on the air as "The Boring Show." One night, John Chancellor, a good friend of Randall's, came by to meet him. Waiting for the show to end, Chancellor and I stood at the bar at the Pla-Mor.

"What's he doing?" Chancellor asked.

"Well John, it is called 'The Boring Show.'"

"They certainly called that right."

The careers of these two friends were entwined through the years. Later, as head of the U.S. Information Agency, John Chancellor hired Randall to work for him. Randall filled various posts, among them Copenhagen, Denmark, and Perth, Australia. He also flew with Lyndon Johnson to Vietnam. In the middle of the night as he was standing watch on board Air Force One, Randall received a call from Washington about a message that had to reach the president. Randall put it in the middle of the president's desk where he knew Johnson would see it. Suddenly he felt an ominous presence, looked up and saw the president standing in the doorway, saying, "Boy, what are you doing messing around my desk?"

———   ———   ———

Randall's finest accomplishment was hiring Sam Feeback as a news photographer. Sam worked many years for WDAF and was a legend among photographers in Kansas City. For one thing, there was his apparel. On assignment he wore a small, brightly colored cap topped with a fuzzy ball. He could identify himself to news sources ahead of time, saying, "You can always find me in a crowd."

Policemen and firemen knew Sam, not only by his hat, but also by his face. He was a former wrestler, once described by a friend as looking like "five miles of bad road." He thought that was funny. Sam covered everything. If he arrived on a fire scene after the blaze was under control, he'd kid the fire chief: "What did you do? You let it go out before I got here?"

He liked to present himself as a something of a redneck, but he was nothing of the kind. Once he covered a house fire on South Benton where four children were left without a parent. When he came back to the station, Sam told everyone the story and showed a picture he had taken as the children stared with sad faces out the window of a neighbor's house. Without telling anyone, Sam went back that afternoon with a station wagon loaded with clothes and toys and delivered them to the house where the children were temporarily quartered. Eventually, a friend told us he had done this, knowing that Sam wouldn't tell us himself.

He became a frequent photographer of Harry S. Truman after the president left office and returned to Independence. Truman would contact Feeback before a news conference and tell him, "Let's go 15 minutes on this." When that time elapsed, Sammie, who was filming the entire news conference, would utter, "Thank you, Mr. President." A year after Truman left office President Eisenhower sent the secretary of state, John Foster Dulles, to Independence to brief Truman. All the press gathered at Municipal airport. The secretary's airplane flew in and stopped in front of the reporters and photographers. John Foster Dulles began his descent down the stairs, waving his hat.

"Sam, are you here?" Dulles said.

"Right here, Mr. Secretary," a voice replied.

"Is this about right for the picture?"

And Sam said, "Yes, just hold it right there for a minute."

After it was over I said, "Sam, where did you ever know John Foster Dulles?" Sam's only response was, "I guess the old man told him to look me up."

Sam had a language all his own. Asked how he got his pictures, he'd say, "I open up, just peeking in, and then I go tippy-toe right up close and just shoot a tweak of this and a tweak of that." What he produced was always excellent and ready for the air. He also loved to say, "Hey, I'm going to a banquet and they're going to give me a reward." The walls of his den were filled with plaques and citations for his work. He would have considered it the greatest "reward" of all to know that he still had the respect of the people in his trade, many years after his death.

In 1953, Sam played a touching role in the wake of the kidnapping of Bobby Greenlease, son of a millionaire Kansas City Cadillac dealer. The boy, 6, was taken from school by a man and woman, who demanded $600,000 in ransom for his return. For days afterward, the kidnappers gave the Greenlease family hope the boy was alive. The ransom was delivered, but it turned out that the couple had killed Bobby within hours of grabbing him. The story made national headlines. The day that Bobby Greenlease was laid to rest, network broadcaster W. W. Chaplin summed up the story this way: "They said the mass of the angels today for 6-year-old Bobby Greenlease, kidnapped for $600,000 ransom and murdered for no reason at all."

During the trial of the two kidnappers, Bonnie Brown Heady, the co-kidnapper, sat at the defendant's table parallel to the press table in the federal courtroom. She seemed to be going out of her way to give one of the reporters a seductive glance. The reporter's response was that he thought he might give up sex for six months. I covered that court proceeding and I will never forget that, as Carl Austin Hall's confession was read, Hall looked for a moment in the direction of Robert Greenlease. For an instant, it seemed, they were joined. The look on Mr. Greenlease's face could be described as anguish. Hall immediately looked away and stared down at the table before him.

Heady and Hall were convicted and sentenced to die in the gas chamber of the Missouri State Prison.

Through all this ordeal, Sam Feeback came to admire the Greenlease family and its courage under terrible duress. He asked to be allowed to dig Hall's grave. That wish was granted and years afterward a photograph hung in Feeback's den at home showing him waist high in the ground, digging the grave of the man he had learned to hate.

In those days, television newscasters sat looking straight into the camera, glancing down at their copy to get a few lines, then looking up to read or ad lib them to the audience. Your eyes went up and down, up and down, all the way through the newscast. If you were unlucky, you'd turn two pages together. Suddenly you'd have jumped ahead from Page 1 to Page 3 and the middle of the story was already lying on the far side of the table.

Visuals were a particular problem. We used small pictures called "telops," usually photos of newsworthy people. For a few seconds, a telop would fill the screen as the announcer kept talking. If something went wrong in the projection room, things could turn out very badly on the air. One night in 1958 I was delivering a story about Charles Starkweather and his girlfriend, 14-year-old Caril Fugate, who were terrorizing Nebraska and Iowa. They were on a rampage of murder, having killed her parents and other people.

"The mad killer of the Midwest is in the news again," I began. Boom, up popped a photo of some up-and-coming politician of the day, grinning. Because you couldn't read copy and watch pictures at the same time, I continued with the story about the couple's bloody journey. Then I went on to the next story: "Meanwhile in the political world a new leader is emerging." Boom, there was Starkweather's picture. A superstition among broadcasters goes like this: Once you begin to crash, you'll crash over and over. If one thing goes wrong, more will follow.

Mixups like that are less common today, yet as long as a television newscast is done live, the potential for trouble remains. Many in the business remember a videotape of a poor sportscaster in Ohio. He was delivering the scores, but everything he called for came up wrong. It was a telecaster's worst nightmare. Finally he put his head down on the table as if to cry. The camera zoomed in for a close-up and that ended sports for that night.

As television progressed, equipment became more sophisticated. In the early days no way existed to instantly play back what you had done. A machine called the kinescope recorded broadcasts from a television monitor on film, but there was a delay while the film was developed, and the quality of reproduction was poor. Still, you could get an idea of how you looked on the air. I remember looking at a kinescope of myself reading the news and seeing my father and my mother, their appearance and their gestures. It was a great revelation. There were others.

While I was anchorman on WDAF television, I occasionally tried to emulate the oratorical style of Franklin D. Roosevelt, whom I admired greatly. When Roosevelt spoke, he'd throw his head from one side to the other to make a special point. I tried that, too. The revelation came to me when I watched myself on the kinescope, throwing my head back and forth and side to side. Why would I do that? I had to mentally glue myself to that conference room chair to keep from walking out. Were my colleagues hoping I'd see how bad this looked? If so, it worked. From that day on I kept my head still. I was surprised they hadn't fired me.

Doing the news was not enough for me.

I talked the bosses into a feature on the midnight news called "Bodine's Midnight Memo." I'd monitor police calls and ride through the city to gather stories. Each story ran about two minutes.

I loved cruising the city for news. One night I turned a corner on Eighth Street, looked through the open door of a dilapidated building and saw a celebration going on inside. On the sidewalk a tiny girl, about 4 years old, was curled up asleep. I quickly made my way to a telephone, reported this to a police dispatcher, then drove around a couple of blocks. By the time I returned, the police were picking up the little girl and taking her inside. I was pretty sure those partygoers were about to hear a lecture on parental responsibility.

My career as a television weathercaster was brief and disastrous. When it happened, one of the the biggest shows on network television was "Mr. Peepers," starring Wally Cox as a mild-mannered teacher. It began on NBC each Sunday night at 6:30 and WDAF scheduled me to do the weather just before it. For the weather commercial, a stagehand would hold up a piece of cardboard with the words. On my first Sunday, feeling nervous, I came on and gave a brief description of the weather, and then said, "I'll give you the full forecast right after this word from Con Frazier Buick." I turned to the stagehand who was holding the commercial cue card, and found he was holding it upside down. Reading upside down on television for a large audience is very difficult, I can assure you. I was beginning to feel the infamous "flop sweat," but I managed somehow to get through. After the commercial, I gave the temperature and got out of the camera's eye. I went over to the stagehand in question, placed my hand on his shoulder and through gritted teeth told him the cue card had been upside down. He was new on the job, which he had received through a relative, and took the matter lightly. I gave him a dirty look and walked away.

On my second Sunday as a weatherman, I came on, gave my tease for the weather and read the commercial. Then I went over to the weather map and took out a huge flow pen to mark on it. I've never cared much about the weather as long as it wasn't life-threatening, but that day I had taken the trouble to learn some things. There was a cold front coming down from the northwest and to show its path I placed the tip of the flow pen on the board. As I pulled it down to draw a black line to show where the front was, no ink came out. Instead, there was a sound reminiscent of fingernails scraping a blackboard.

There's a superstition that bad things come in threes, and once again I went to the stagehand, saying: "I don't want you to take this personally but if there is no ink in that pen when I come back next time, I will throttle you. And I hope you will take that as a threat." Again he took it as a joke. Somehow I knew my career as a weathercaster was about to end.

The third Sunday, I came downstairs early and said to the stagehand:

"Let me see the commercial. You're going to hold it up right; please look at it when you put it out there."

"Sure," he said.

I checked everything.

"Is there ink in that flow pen?"

"Yeah, sure."

With a full week to prepare, it seemed that this time I was set to do the thing right. I had rehearsed carefully. Then came time, and that big audience was out there once again. I did the tease, and the commercial and then a spiel about the weather and how once again we had a situation with a cold front moving in on us. I turned, picked up the flow pen, and placed it at the top to draw the line. As I pressed it to the board, ink came out in a mighty flow, obliterating Montana and parts of Utah and Nebraska. I turned around and tried to block the camera's view of most of the mess, trying to remember what I would be saying if I didn't have the map. That was the longest five minutes I could remember.

Albert Einstein has been quoted as saying that an hour sitting with a pretty girl is like a minute, but a minute sitting on a hot stove is like an hour. It was clear that I was not destined to be the Einstein of weathermen. I met with the general manager, Bill Bates, on Monday.

"I don't know what else can happen to this weather show," I told him, "but it isn't going to be on my watch. I've screwed it up enough." A successor was appointed, and I was never so happy to lose a job. I went back to being a newscaster, and most folks were kind enough never to mention the matter again. As for that stagehand, he finally figured out that television was a serious business and became quite good at his tasks.

WDAF had a weekly live program called "Kansas City Live," which aired for an hour every Friday. Once I participated in a segment about stock-car racing, shot at a track in Riverside. Owen Bush, a WDAF sportscaster, drove one of the cars, and I drove another. I had never sat in such a contraption. Among other things, it had no windshield. To demonstrate the excitement of the sport, the two of us raced our cars around the track. We ran neck-and-neck, and as I rounded the first turn I thought about my wife and five children.

"If I crack up here," I wondered, "will my insurance be any good?"

But I continued along at what seemed breakneck speed. We came around the bend to the finish line at almost exactly the same time. Once across, we emerged from the cars and felt quite proud of ourselves. Then we returned to the station and watched a taped playback.

"It would take a pair of great-grandmothers," one wag said, "to poke along that slow on a racetrack." Indeed, it looked like we were on the boulevard doing about 35 miles an hour. I emerged with new respect for racecar drivers.

When Randall Jessee left WDAF-TV in 1958, I became the news director and Bill Leeds the assistant news director. We worked side-by-side every night. Even as television grew in sophistication, there was still room for horseplay. It wasn't quite the same as the tricks we played at the little station in Atchison — no firecrackers for us. We had other ways.

If I found a funny or bizarre story on the Associated Press wire, I'd keep it out of Bill's sight until he was nearing his last report. Then I'd have the story placed in front of him to see whether he would crack up. That proved difficult. Usually, he was too professional to let it happen. One day I found a story that did the trick. There was a man in the East, according to this news item, who had gone to court to request a name change. His name was Joe Stinks and he wanted it changed to William Stinks. When

Leeds hit that line, he laughed so hard he had to put his head down and throw the show back to me. I smiled as we went off the air.

Years earlier, on WDAF radio, Bill and I were doing our daily 5 p.m. drive-time news. We read our news stories in rotation. At the end, one of us would read the weather and the other would say, "And that's the 5 o'clock news. This is Walt Bodine…and this is Bill Leeds." One day in particular I was not doing well. It was one of those days when I simply couldn't talk straight, a terrible feeling. On days like that, if you flub a line at the start of a newscast, you try hard not to make more mistakes. Because of that, you become nervous and mistakes pile up. After many muddles, we reached the end and I thought my only salvation was to play a joke on Bill. So as we came to the sign-off, I said, "And that's the news at 5. This is Bill Leeds…." Leeds gave me a startled look, recovered and said very quietly, "and this is Walt Bodine." We did that to keep our sanity.

It's been a long time since I've seen this kind of humor behind the scenes or on the air. The news these days maintains a strictly corporate look.

Sometimes there were dramatic moments in the old newsroom at WDAF-TV that had nothing to do with the newscast. In the 1950s our studios on Signal Hill were among the newest and biggest between Chicago and the West Coast, and we occasionally originated national broadcasts when the performers' schedules made it necessary. One week the show was "Coke Time with Eddie Fisher," which would take place in our studio and be fed to the NBC Network. Fisher and his wife, Debbie Reynolds, were both in town. Right then news came over our business wire that the Coca-Cola Company was replacing its advertising agency — the very agency that had arranged Coke's sponsorship of the Eddie Fisher program. With a new agency usually came a new strategy, so it was almost a given that things were going to change. Often that meant sponsored shows would be canceled.

We called someone from the show's production staff, who took one look at the story and turned pale.

"I'd better go downstairs and tell them about it," he said. He shared the news with the rest of the crew and a few minutes later Debbie Reynolds and Eddie Fisher came into the newsroom, arm in arm. As they read the news, I saw Debbie Reynolds move over, take Fisher's hand and hold it tight. It was a touching scene. One day you can be the the toast of the town, and the next day fearing for your job.

On a warm August morning in 1959, when I was news director of WDAF television and radio, I was driving to my office when the police radio reported that there was a fire at a gasoline and kerosene storage facility on Southwest Boulevard at 31st Street. That was right at the state line and only a few blocks from the station. After calling work, I switched my radio over to WDAF and heard reporter John Harrington, who had arrived on the scene and was broadcasting a description of the fire. It had been going on for a while. With traffic blocked, firemen knelt in the middle of Southwest Boulevard, aiming streams of water at the blaze. I arrived, saw a battalion chief nearby and left my car to talk to him. Suddenly we heard a high, whistling sound.

"What's that?" I asked the chief.

"I'm not sure," he said, "but I don't like the sound of it."

He began walking toward the street and moments later the tanks exploded, shooting a wall of flame across Southwest Boulevard straight at the firefighters. Harrington continued to describe the horrible scene, his voice becoming tenser by the moment. At the height of emotion, nearly breathless as it became clear that firemen had been overtaken by the flame, he said, "Take it, Walt, take it."

Like Harrington, I was horrified. We could see men running, their clothes on fire, trying to escape. The shock of the sight had nearly stopped me from talking when suddenly a little voice in my head said, "It's only a movie." Surely I'd heard that phrase many times from my parents when we would go to a disturbing show, but under these very different and very real circumstances it still somehow kicked in. Because of it, I was able to stay calm and report what I saw.

What I saw was men dying fiery deaths and eventually ambulances lining up at the scene, like taxis at the airport. Five firefighters and a volunteer died in the explosion, and scores of firemen were injured.

I radioed the newsroom to send staffers to the hospitals, asking them to gather an entire list of injured firemen for the 12:30 p.m. news, which was only a couple hours away. The families of firemen were living through a terrible morning, waiting for news about their loved ones. Working hard and covering the hospitals thoroughly, WDAF staffers were able to compile a complete list of the injured for the early afternoon broadcast.

The story had multiple angles, and we had to do a feed for the early evening NBC news, so it wasn't until about 4 p.m. that I could take a breather. All of a sudden the magnitude of what I had witnessed kicked in. No longer was there a little voice telling me, "It's OK, it's only a movie."   Reality was back, but the ability to think of the event as unreal got me through that day.

One month later, in September 1959, I took a crew to Des Moines to cover Nikita Khrushchev, the leader of the Soviet Union and the ultimate symbol of our greatest Cold War foe. On the way to Des Moines in the station's cruiser, we tuned in a talk show in which people were being interviewed on the street. The host, Russ Van Dyne, asked one woman whether she was going to watch Khrushchev arrive in Des Moines.

No, she replied, she'd look for him as he made his way to the farm of Roswell Garst out in the country. "It will take him on a highway that runs just behind my house," she said. "I'll wait by the fence and watch the motorcade go by."

And then she added, "After all, you know, he may not pass this way again."

Indeed. We laughed so hard we almost drove off the highway.

The scene around the Hotel Fort Des Moines, where Khrushchev was to arrive, showed that he was probably the best-protected person in the world that day. The Secret Service, FBI, local police, and others were in the streets and on all the rooftops. The press corps, meanwhile, was quarrelsome because we were being kept 30 feet from the entrance to the hotel. Salt was rubbed in our wound when Khrushchev alighted from his limousine under the hotel marquee. As all the professional photographers strained to take photos from behind security ropes, a Kansas City doctor, D.M. Nigro — whose trademark was taking photographs of anyone he saw and mailing the picture to them — stepped out of the hotel just as Khrushchev began walking toward the door. Nigro smiled, Khrushchev stopped and smiled back and the doctor snapped his picture. "How did he *do* that?" the press photographers asked, angrily and enviously.

The   next day, we headed for the Garst farm near Coon Rapids, about 70 miles west of Des Moines. Down the highway, we found an open spot and pulled over next to a field, waiting to watch the motorcade pass. The line of cars came into view and then, to our amazement, Krushchev's limousine pulled up and stopped right in front of us.

The back door swung open and out stepped Nikita Khrushchev, leader of the Soviet Union, wearing a tan suit with a star hanging from the breast pocket, and flashing a wide smile. Had he mistaken us for the welcoming party? We were stunned. This beaming man standing next to us on the roadside was the biggest news story on earth that day. We called ourselves reporters, but we couldn't imagine what to do with him except smile back.

Suddenly we heard chattering in Russian coming from the

radio of the limousine. One of his aides guided Khrushchev back to his seat, closed the doors and the motorcade sped away. We stood there dumbfounded, watching the limousine disappear.

Once at the Garst farm we mingled with some of the celebrities and Khrushchev. Soviet and U.S. officials walked between rows of Iowa corn, followed by the large press corps. The tall, dignified Henry Cabot Lodge — a Boston Brahmin who was then U.S. ambassador to the United Nations — was as improbable a person as you'd ever expect to see in a cornfield. We trailed behind Khrushchev and the rest as Garst guided them through his fields. Finally, Garst got annoyed with the press corps. He leaned over, picked up a handful of silage — chopped corn — and threw it at a batch of photographers. Khrushchev looked on, smiling. The photographers captured the moment and many of us appeared the next day on America's front pages, laughing and ducking silage.

INTERLUDE

Media and Reality

People often mix up the fictional and the real.
That came home to me one night when I was
covering a circus at the Municipal Auditorium.
When I arrived at one of the big entrances on the side
of the building I came upon three or four high school
girls watching the show. On one side, elephants were
performing, in the center ring clowns were piling out
of a Volkswagen, and on the other side acrobats were
doing their tricks.

"Gee, this is just like Cinerama!" one of the
girls said.

People measure the real by fiction.

*   *   *

In the late 1950s, when I worked at WDAF and
did a midnight news show, Lee Marvin came to town
to promote his television series, "M-Squad." In it he
played Lieutenant Frank Ballinger of the Chicago
Police Department. Marvin went along with me as I

cruised the city looking for an item for "Bodine's Midnight Memo." As we rode, he spent most of the time telling me in no uncertain terms how much he hated the Chicago cops. With 11:30 approaching I was getting nervous because there had been nothing to report. Then came a call that there'd been a holdup at a pawn shop on Main Street. It took us seven or eight minutes to get there, and Kansas City police investigators already were on the scene. The woman who ran the pawn shop was giving a description of the robbers to a policeman when we walked in. Immediately she swept aside the real policeman and ran over to Lee Marvin.

"Lieutenant," she told him, "these two guys just came in here and robbed me." She reported the whole story to the actor who only *portrayed* a cop. The real policemen were somewhat amused. After we returned to the car, Marvin said: "Believe it or not, that's not the first time that happened."

*   *   *

This phenomenon of the real and the unreal has manifested itself in many ways around broadcasters. One day Randall Jesse was shopping in a grocery near the television station when he noticed a woman staring at him. He thought nothing of it and left for home. The next time Randall went in the store, the grocer said: "Hey, do you remember the last time you were in the store and that lady was staring at you? Do you know what she said after you left? She said: 'All this time I've been watching him. The least he could have done is give me a big smile and come over and talk to me.' " That was in the early days of television, when to many viewers the medium was still something of a mystery.

On another occasion a woman called Randall at the station and said: "I watch you every night and enjoy seeing you so much. I wanted you to know that I bought a new gown just for you. How do you like it?"

*   *   *

Years later, after television had become commonplace, I participated in another reality check. At the student union at the University of Missouri-Kansas City, I noticed that a lot of students gathered at midday, doing some homework and watching the soap opera "All My Children." One of the stars was a well-known movie actress, Ruth Warrick, who played the part of Phoebe Tyler Wallingford. She was born in St. Joseph, later moved to Kansas City and had graduated from the University of Kansas City, which became UMKC. She happened to be in town and was scheduled to appear on my talk show, and it struck me that we could do something interesting. I arranged with her to arrive at the UMKC student union about 10 minutes into an episode of "All My Children."

As usual, a band of students was watching the show intently when all of a sudden Phoebe Tyler Wallingford, dressed as she was on the show, walked over to the television set and stood beside it. For 15 seconds there was a total lack of reaction, and then in the back row a girl exclaimed, "Oh, my God!" Quickly a medley of sounds signaled the group's dismay. They stared at her as if she had just stepped right out of the television set. Ruth Warrick looked at them, turned off the set and said in her best scolding voice: "What on earth are you doing watching stuff like that? You're here to study and prepare yourself for life. You can't learn anything from this trash."

Just then, I walked out and said, "That's startling, isn't it? Phoebe Tyler Wallingford came right out of the television. We're doing this to see how you'd react to someone from the make-believe world of television materializing as a real person."

I introduced her and told them that she was a distinguished graduate of the university's theater program and that she had appeared in movies, one of them playing the role of Charles Foster Kane's first wife in "Citizen Kane."

The students gathered around her to talk, but

even though we had revealed her real identity, to
them she remained Phoebe Tyler Wallingford. They
asked Phoebe, not Ruth, questions about the
characters in the soap opera as if every character
were alive and real. As we were leaving, she told me
a person had approached her in New York one day
and warned her to watch out for another character on
the show. Sometimes it's difficult for people to
discern what is fiction and what is not.

*   *   *

The endless conflict between the real world and
the world of fiction affects me the same way. When
The Hustler came out in theaters, I watched the
powerful and memorable portrayal of Minnesota Fats
by Jackie Gleason. Years later, when I booked the real
Minnesota Fats on WHB, I was shocked to find he
didn't look or sound like Jackie Gleason. He was a
nice man and we did a good show, but somehow I
resented him because he upset my vision of what he
was supposed to be. When the show was over and
he was on his way out the door I kept saying to
myself — against all evidence to the contrary — there
goes an imposter!

Presidents

Kansas City has always been a pretty good place for president-watching. Without leaving Kansas City, I've seen nine presidents of the United States, interviewed some, shaken hands with others and observed the back of Jimmy Carter's head. Maybe I should make the count 8 1/2.

Harry S. Truman

Before I ever met him, I encountered Harry S. Truman's salty tongue indirectly.

While Truman was in office, he took plenty of criticism from the press and finally had it up to here with one journalist, Drew Pearson. On a radio broadcast, Pearson had complained about Truman's military aide, Harry Vaughan. In response, Truman declared that no "S.O.B.," could force the president to do something by making some "some smart-aleck announcement over the air." The epithet "S.O.B." presented a dilemma to newsrooms all over the country. For me the question was, "Can I say this over the radio?" Nobody was more under the gun than I was, facing a 10 p.m. newscast on WDAF radio less than half an hour from the time the news came over the teletype. By the standards of the late 1940s, "S.O.B." was bad enough. But had he really uttered

the full term? I called downstairs and got one of the
night editors on the newspaper city desk. In those
days, *The Star* owned WDAF and we worked in the
same building.

"What about this Truman story?" I asked. "Are
you going to use the quote? I need to know because
I'm going on the air in a few minutes." No matter
what he answered I wasn't sure whether we in
broadcasting, subject to federal supervision, could go
as far as the print media. The night editor referred
me to someone else and I started going up the ladder.
Finally I reached the top man on duty that night, who
at first thought it was funny, but he wasn't sure what
the newspaper was going to do. Finally, he said that
I would have to call the boss, Roy Roberts, president
of the company. A few moments later I was talking
to him.

"Mr. Roberts, this is Walt Bodine at the radio
station," I said. "We have something on the
Associated Press tonight that quotes President
Truman as using 'S.O.B.' in reference to Drew
Pearson. The question is, Do you think that's OK to
use on the radio?" Roberts thought for a moment or
two and said: "Do you think he really just said,
'S.O.B.' or did he say, `son of a bitch'? If he did, I
wouldn't suggest using the direct quote, but if the AP
chose to use it with those three letters, which
everybody understands...." He paused for a moment

and then said, "Yup, just go with it." So the decision was made and I aired it.

For the next few days, yowling and howling came from listeners, several of whom were not known for their love of President Truman. I heard men I knew personally — any one of whom could rival a sea captain at cursing — express outrage that such language could be used by a president and end up in print and on the air. Truman, who had been bombarded by political and journalistic enemies before, knew that all he had to do was wait it out. I have a feeling he enjoyed it.

Today, of course, most broadcasters wouldn't hesitate to cite the president's words.

*   *   *

My first encounter with Truman was at an event at the Hotel Muehlebach shortly after he returned from Washington in 1953. As the crowd moved around him, I finally found myself near him. I stepped up in front of him and we exchanged pleasantries. I don't remember what was said but I have a keen memory of his eyes — large, blue eyes behind his thick glasses. He made you feel he was giving you his full attention.

*   *   *

One night in the mid-50s I was assigned to go in a chauffeured limousine to the World War II Memorial Building at Linwood Boulevard and Paseo to pick up Mr. and Mrs. Truman and bring them back to WDAF, where the former president was to appear on an NBC show. As I came into the hall, Truman was trying to work his way quickly to the door, shaking hands as he went along. I guided him and Bess Truman to the back seat of the limo — a class of vehicle used in those days primarily by funeral homes — and sat facing them on a jump seat. As we drove I said to them, "You know it's wonderful to be riding in a car like this without somebody being dead." Mrs. Truman, especially, thought that was a hoot. We made it to the station with only a few minutes to spare.

*   *   *

I watched him work crowds many times. People were forever saying: "You were a great president. I wish you were back in Washington now." When people told him that he had been a great chief executive he'd say, "We'll have to wait 50 years and let history decide." It has been 50 years and history has shown that Truman was, indeed, one of the great presidents.

*   *   *

When the Truman Library was opening in

Independence, I was allowed to wander through with others from the news media. I paused at the wonderful, exact replica of the Oval Office as it had been in the Truman era. Truman's desk was there with the sign, "The Buck Stops Here." On a side wall of the office an opening had been made, allowing people to step inside in front of a small barrier. About the time I stepped in, Truman came in and sat down behind the desk. He was followed by his former secretary of state, Dean Acheson, who slipped easily into the chair beside Truman. They began to talk quietly and confidentially. About that time, two women stepped in and looked at Truman and Acheson. As they came out, one of the visitors said: "Did you see how true to life they looked? It's almost as if they were really there."

*   *   *

In those days, a presidential visit to the Muehlebach Hotel was no secret to anyone in the vicinity. Along the curb, police motorcycles were parked in military formation ready to pull away at a moment's notice. The presidential limousine was there with its flags mounted on the fenders. When President Truman entered the hotel, the manager, Barney Allis, saw to it that the bellhops were standing on both sides of the steps with white gloves, greeting the president as he went up the stairs where he caught the elevator to the presidential suite.

Dwight D. Eisenhower

In all the times I saw Eisenhower, I never saw the famous Eisenhower grin.

Just before he accepted the Republican nomination for president, he made a visit to Kansas City, Kansas, and spoke at a luncheon. What I recall was that he seemed to be somewhat red of face, and I hoped this potential president was not having blood-pressure problems.

I didn't see him again until a winter day in early 1958. Eisenhower was flying to Kansas City for the funeral of his brother, Arthur B. Eisenhower, who was a banker here.

The president's plane was scheduled to land at Municipal airport, and the press gathered there. But a heavy ground fog had set in, and word soon spread that his plane would be diverted to another airport, perhaps Richards-Gebauer. Before we could head that way we heard on the police radio that he would land at the Olathe Naval Air Station near Gardner in Johnson County. So we sped southwest.

Plans had changed so quickly that top-ranking officers of the air station were not around. Nevertheless, an old U.S. Navy Chevrolet with "U.S. Navy For Official Use Only" stenciled on the side was quickly secured. As we watched the president climb into the back seat, one of the members of the press said, "That's about the most lowly vehicle he's ridden in for a long time." The motorcade left, escorted by Olathe police and Kansas troopers. We followed at speeds as high as 80 miles an hour. As the motorcade raced north, it seemed that every corner had a policeman holding back traffic. The president stopped briefly at his brother's home on Ensley Lane in Mission Hills. While Eisenhower went inside to talk to his brother's widow, Press Secretary Jim Haggerty, a man whose name we saw daily on teletype wires, stood by the curb, kicking a few leaves around. When the president emerged, the motorcade continued to the Stine & McClure Chapel on Gillham Plaza south of Linwood.

*   *   *

My strongest memory of Eisenhower was at the end of his life in 1969. Along with a handful of other reporters, we stood in the middle of the night under the railroad sheds at Union Station. In the distance finally, we heard the bell of a train — ding ... ding ... ding. It was the funeral train of Dwight D. Eisenhower, headed home to Abilene for the last time.

The train pulled in and came to a stop so the engine and crew could be changed. Through a window of the first car, we could see the flag-draped

coffin of the man who led Allied forces to victory in
Europe in World War II. A man riding with Mamie
Eisenhower stepped off and asked everyone to be
quiet. We figured Mrs. Eisenhower was asleep.
Later, the train again sounded its bell and pulled out
of Union Station, headed west, where Eisenhower
completed his life cycle on the grounds of the
Eisenhower Presidential Library in Abilene, the place
of his boyhood.

John F. Kennedy

In early 1960 I was summoned, along with Chris
Condon, another reporter at WDAF television, to the
Town House Hotel in Kansas City, Kansas, to
interview John F. Kennedy, who was then running for
president. Along with us went David Oestreicher of
United Press International's Kansas City bureau.
When we arrived, Kennedy sat down in a rocking
chair and we began asking questions. In the middle
of that UPI in New York called Oestreicher to the
phone, wanting a story for deadline. Oestreicher
began dictating: "John F. Kennedy, Roman Catholic
candidate for president...." Kennedy broke off
suddenly in the middle of what he was saying to the
rest of us.

"Excuse me," he said, turning around. "Mr.
Oestreicher...Mr. Oestreicher?" David stopped and
said, "Yes, Senator?" And Kennedy said, "I was just

listening to your opening. Do you think that's fair? I am a Roman Catholic, but I'm not running as a Catholic candidate for president. I am a Democratic candidate for president."

Oestreicher said, "Yes, Senator, you're right." He changed his story. In the meantime, Senator Kennedy turned back to us and took up right where he had left off. I thought it was remarkable that a man could simultaneously talk to the press and hear what another reporter was saying across the room.

Why was JFK speaking to us at the Town House Hotel in Kansas City, Kansas? He came to counties where there was a sizable Democratic vote, and one of those was Wyandotte County. I'm sure he also visited Sedgwick County. We were told that he stopped in Hays, Kansas, in Ellis County. "That's solid Republican territory out there, isn't it?" I asked an aide. "All but Hays," the aide replied. "For some reason Hays, Kansas, has usually voted Democratic."

I followed Kennedy through that campaign and was assigned to the 1960 Democratic Convention in Los Angeles. I remember crouching in one of the aisles close up, watching Kennedy delivering his acceptance speech. Members of the Kennedy clan and Lyndon B. Johnson and his family were gathered on the platform. It was a wildly exciting political moment.

*   *   *

A month after his nomination, Kennedy came to Kansas City to meet with Truman at the Muehlebach Hotel. Kennedy suggested they go down to one of the halls in the hotel where a big union convention was under way. To the great surprise of the delegates to that convention, the doors opened and in walked Truman and the newly nominated John F. Kennedy. They socialized with the delegates and answered serious questions. When they left Truman accompanied Kennedy into the lobby of the Muehlebach, where they parted. Kennedy walked across a roped-off area of the lobby to go to his car. A woman's hand came out from a group of people behind the ropes and grabbed Kennedy's arm, almost knocking him over. Announcing she was from Dallas, Texas, she said, "I hope you will come down sometime and see us." He flashed her a winning smile and said, "Thank you, I'll try to do that." On the day the fatal shots were fired that took his life, I remembered that moment and that woman.

*　　*　　*

President Kennedy held unprecedented media sessions with a special focus on television and radio. With previous presidents, newspaper reporters got first crack, but Kennedy seemed attuned to the important role of broadcasting in politics. The Kennedy Administration held week-long foreign policy briefings once and sometimes twice a year, and I was one of the reporters chosen to spend a week at the State Department. If the issue was, for example, nuclear weapons, all the top players in that field took part in a day-long session for the media. One unusually good briefing was given by the State Department's undersecretary for African affairs, G. Mennen Williams, the former governor of Michigan. He covered an area we still don't thoroughly understand in the West and told of the enormous number of languages and other complexities of the African continent. In early November 1963, I attended one of these briefings, and when we returned from lunch, the first thing we did was glance at the rostrum. If the presidential seal was there, it meant Kennedy soon would be, too. It was there, and soon he was talking to us and taking questions from the floor. I couldn't help but think that Kennedy seemed more like a friend than a father or grandfather, the way his predecessors had. He looked vigorous and tanned and fielded questions with a quick wit. This, I thought, was a remarkable man in his prime. Only a few weeks later he was gunned down in Dallas.

Have I Mentioned Food?

One place I wish could be brought back to life, if only for one more meal, is the marvelous Forum Cafeteria on Main Street downtown. You could dine there and then catch the twilight show at the beautiful Loew's Midland Theatre a couple of doors down. When we were staff announcers at WDAF, I used to dine with Charles Bebb, whom we called "Chow Mein" Bebb because of his love for the Forum's version of that item. Almost everyone had a favorite dish at the Forum. People stood in long lines just to get in. Usually I'd top off my meal with Boston cream pie with whipped cream piled high on top. I've since given up on Boston cream pie, because I've already had the best.

*   *   *

The Joe Gilbert restaurant at Municipal airport was a 24-hour feast with excellent food and a great chance to watch celebrities as they came through town or changed planes. When I had a late-night talk show, I often ate a delayed dinner there. Once, I saw Bing Crosby and Bob Hope in a single booth. Another time, I heard someone with a familiar voice ordering coffee right beside me. I turned for a look and it was Peter Lorre in a Homburg. One night at

the airport I ran into Gary Cooper, who had unbelievably blue eyes. In his best western style, he said, "Howdy." I said, "Howdy."

After finishing my dinner about 2 a.m. one night I noticed a little group standing around a pinball machine. Playing it was Elvis Presley, and the folks surrounding him evidently were his bodyguards. Whenever he lost, he simply extended his hand and one of the bodyguards gave him a coin to continue.

*   *   *

Roy Herndon, who worked at the Robinson drugstore at 34th and Main streets, could produce a chocolate malt I have never seen equaled. What's more, he had a sense of style, and the malt was served with a can of nutmeg. Some nights, if you were lucky, he would have brought from home some wonderful roast beef prepared by his wife.

*   *   *

One of the best hamburgers I've eaten was served at the drive-in at 44th and Main streets operated for years by Roy Cone and Ray Shannon. Their Southside hamburger was a respectable-sized patty with a generous portion of onion rings on top. I ate each one lovingly.

*   *   *

Thursdays the lunch special at Max Bretton's restaurant in the 1200 block of Baltimore was beef stroganoff. On one occasion I ate two orders of it while my talk-show partner, Jean Glenn, shook her head in disbelief.

*   *   *

And how can I forget...
• King Joy Lo's, upstairs at 12th and Main, with windows overlooking the street. There you could dine and people-watch at the same time, and the egg foo yung made other Asian chefs try harder.
• The Country Club Dairy ice cream store at 56th and Troost. You could eat at a table, a booth, or the counter.
• Macaroni and cheese and spinach salad at Putsch's cafeterias.
• Wonderful breakfasts in the old Alameda Hotel.
• Breakfast in the Westport Room in Union Station. The Fred Harvey company proved throughout a 24-hour day that it deserved its reputation for great food.

Bodine's Bailiwick

A regular column on the air broadcast weekdays on
WDAF radio. This one was from October 7, 1957.

This is sort of a grumpish ode to the most varicose day of the week. They call it Monday, but actually the word Monday is almost too good for it.

Monday. Almost anything or anyone is too good for it, but it's necessary to put up with Monday to get from Sunday to Tuesday. We have to put up with it just like you used to have to put up with the old Hannibal Bridge if you wanted to get to the airport. The only difference is, we built a new bridge. But Monday…. Well, it goes forever.

What is Monday? Monday is the sort of a day when you must carry out a resolve to begin dieting. All weekend long you nibble at icebox goodies or treat yourself to one more chocolate cookie, promising all the while to make up for it Monday. Monday you start dieting. Monday you kill your taste buds with a hard freeze. Monday.

Monday is when you have to cope with whatever you weren't up to on Friday. The only difference is that you are proportionately less able to cope with it according to the riotousness of the weekend. With only a few short hours of sleep you are supposed to separate the mellow, relaxed ways of a suburban squire from the evil demands of the high-pressure business world — the world of annual reports and deadlines, and of tackling that tough appointment. That hard job that has to be done at home or office is today a vulture on your shoulder.

Good old Monday.

Monday. That's the day when you're going to be up and at 'em. Boy, you can hardly wait to get started — on Friday — but now the words, "This is it" sound about as unwelcome as they do to a G.I. in a trench.

What is Monday? Monday is a miniature of the first day after vacation. If you work in an office, Monday is the day that some fool keeps moving the typewriter keys before you can hit them. It is also the day when you get to change the typewriter ribbon that looked OK for one more day on Friday.

Monday is when the boss wants to write double the daily quota of letters because he goofed off on the golf course last week. And Monday is also when his secretary can only take half the usual quota of letters because she was playing too late the night before.

That's the sneaky thing about Monday. You stay up past midnight Sunday and meet Monday that way, and it seems like a perfectly lovely day. Why, Monday at 12:02 a.m. or even 1 a.m. is a time of lovely adventure. But when you turn your back on it briefly for a few moments' sleep, Monday turns on you like a wildcat coming down with the Asian flu.

But that's Monday. Monday is the day when people from lost weekends get found — and found out.

Monday is a long list of unpleasantries written on a desk calendar back when they could still be postponed. Saturday night was when you were going to write to your congressman about some outrage. Monday is when you'd do it if you could just remember what outrage it was, and the only outrage you can think of is — Monday.

Monday is a joke with no punch-line. Monday is when the little dimpled darlings who slept angelically last night just stopped sleeping. Now look at them. When the same little darlings have an oatmeal fight and set up a series of howls that would do credit to a prison riot — that's right, dearie, that's Monday morning.

Monday morning is also the day when you remember your briefcase on the bookcase after you're halfway downtown. And if you go back you'll probably pick up and lug to work the bookcase instead of the briefcase.

Monday is when the midget wayfarers stand glumly at the curb and wait for the school bus — with the same expressions their daddies once wore waiting for a troop ship going the wrong way.

Monday is when the man who decided to get along without Miltowns last Thursday or so decides he'd better have just one more today.

Monday.

You know how morning disc jockeys, and waitresses where you eat breakfast, and a few others can still seem so bright? They've lost track. They think it's Tuesday.

Monday. Seven-to-one odds against everything....

Oh well, there's nothing wrong with Monday that Tuesday can't cure, I guess.

Wednesday, anyone?

C H A P T E R   V

"Conversation" - Tony Bennett, Rock Hudson, Julie London, Jonas Salk and More - "Insight" - Pierre Salinger, Martin Luther King Jr. - Thomas Hart Benton's Furnace - Leaving WDAF

A new direction opened for me in 1960, the talk show, and for most of my life since I've stayed on that course. In the early days of my talk-show career, I handled news, too, but I was beginning to weary of it. Sometimes I felt like the veteran New York editor who said that news was just the same old stuff happening to different people. On talk shows, you had a better chance of hearing firsthand from listeners, no longer having to guess who they were and what they wanted to know.

It was in 1960 that WDAF radio launched "Conversation," which originated at Bretton's Restaurant on Baltimore Avenue downtown.

Our studio was a front table by the windows. My co-host, Jean Glenn, looking bright and beautiful, sat across from me. Between us sat the guest of the day for an hourlong show that went on the air about 1 p.m. Bretton's was a great place for it, right across the street from the Muehlebach Hotel. At that time, almost every celebrity who came through Kansas City stayed at the Muehlebach, and Bretton's was one of the city's best restaurants. Max Bretton, a one-time rabbi, presided. He knew food and made sure that it was wonderfully prepared.

Our list of guests included Lyndon B. Johnson as senator and as nominee for vice president, Bobby Kennedy when he was working for his brother's presidential campaign, James Michener recalling his first book, and Julie London, Margaret Mead, Norman Vincent Peale, Werner Von Braun and Rock Hudson. The variety was terrific. We had the "hoodlum priest," Charles Dismas Clark of St. Louis, who ministered to ex-convicts, and Nathan Leopold, who had served more than three decades in prison for the murder of Chicago teenager Bobby Franks.

In a live show you found out who was a trouper. One hot summer day Homer Wadsworth, a former educator who for decades headed the Kansas City Association of Trusts and Foundations, was seated ready to go on the air. I moved my microphone, knocked over a pitcher and spilled ice water into our guest's lap. Just then I was saying: "Good afternoon. Welcome to 'Conversation' with Jean Glenn and Walt Bodine...and our guest today, Homer Wadsworth." Homer never missed a beat. He even forgave me when the show was over.

Tony Bennett joined us when he came to town. He was an easygoing guy with a good sense of humor, and he and I found something in common almost immediately. Tony Bennett had worked in his father's grocery in New York, just as I had worked in my father's drugstore in Kansas City. Both of us had to use a white chalklike substance to write messages on the glass windows, advertising the store's specials. Both of us came under criticism from our fathers for our spelling failures. Tony Bennett's nemesis was "cauliflower." I had once written "aspern—24 cents" on the window of Bodine's drugstore. Tony Bennett's career went a long way and I'd like to think that never again did he have to worry about how to spell "cauliflower."

"Conversation" drew a large radio audience, including legions of young, college-trained women who were housebound while raising families. Many tried to keep up with literature. For them we offered guests like James Michener, who told us how he had considered settings that hadn't been overworked by other authors when he produced his first book, *Tales of the South Pacific*. I asked him, "If you were a young man starting out and you couldn't be a writer, what would be your most promising field?" He replied, "A space lawyer." He was quite certain that legal problems were going to arise there, and that space law probably would turn out to be a lucrative and interesting profession. Maybe someday….

The singer and actress Julie London wore a low-necked dress the day she was our guest, and she looked attractive. Clearly, however, she was not charmed at being routed out so early for lunch and an hourlong interview. About halfway through a difficult show, I glanced over and to my dismay saw that Miss London's microphone — a lavaliere-style mike, attached like a necklace — had come unfastened. Slowly, the mike was sliding down into her cleavage. I tried my partner: "Jean, I think Julie is having a little trouble with her microphone. Could you reach over and help her?"

"No," Jean replied, flashing an impish smile. "You go right ahead."

Not wishing to retrieve it by hand, I did the best I could.

"Miss London, I think we are having a problem with your microphone," I told her. "Right now, we don't know whether we are getting a radio show with you or an electrocardiogram." As she sat there looking mystified our engineer, Bill Godden, hurried around the table and refastened the mike.

Another day on "Conversation" we had rocket expert Werner Von Braun. I mentioned that American boys were intrigued with rocket travel and spent a lot of time reading *Popular Mechanics* and *Popular Science*. He said he had read magazines like those in his own youth in Germany, adding, "There's no doubt they created a life-long interest for me in space and space travel." We agreed that the most interesting stories in those publications concerned innovative transportation of the future, things such as monorails and passenger-carrying rockets. It was our tough luck that freeways and subways had become far more common.

Giselle MacKenzie, famous for her appearances on "Your Hit Parade" was on the show when she was in Kansas City appearing at the Starlight Theatre. Singing in outdoor theaters, she confessed, was difficult because of the bugs. A singer had to keep going even if a bug landed in her open mouth.

"I swallowed them all bravely," she said, "but please, no june bugs."

122

In an interview with Margaret Mead I tossed out a reference to the rat race that so many of us felt we were in.

"Young man," the renowned anthropologist told me, "we are humans, not rats." She complimented Kansas City: "You know what I like here? You have lots and lots of parks and smaller green spaces. That's lacking in New York where I come from.

"If a man and woman have a quarrel and one of them goes out of the apartment and slams the door and they go downstairs, there is the world rushing by, not interested in his or her problem. If anything, it just might make the situation worse. Here you could walk a block or two, come to a little park with a bench and sit down and think it over."

One day we announced that the next day's guest was going to be Rock Hudson, then an idol of many women. They crowded into Bretton's for his interview. I had never seen so many white gloves. Dressed to the nines, they filled all the tables so they could say they'd had lunch with the handsome star. They listened carefully to everything going on at our table, but Rock didn't have a lot to say that day. He wasn't at ease with the talk-show format, and was shy, anyway.

Jean and I tried everything to get him into an area where he was comfortable. We talked to each other about his movies, hoping to draw him out. Nothing worked. In desperation I said: "I'll bet in making a movie, as tense as it is, you have to have a sense of humor. I'll bet some funny things happen now and then, don't they?" He thought a while — it seemed like four minutes —

and said, "Well, I can't think of one." Finally he recalled this incident: "Once I was leaning against a false marble column and the darn thing fell over." I guess you had to be there, I thought, holding my tongue.

Another difficult guest was Edward Everett Horton, who had starred in comic roles in many a movie. On our show he was very nervous. Just before we went on the air he said to Jean and me: "I want you to understand I am a comic actor, not a comic. I never say or do anything funny when I'm not doing it in connection with a performance. I'm normally a quiet and private person. A comic can sit here and banter with you for a whole hour, but I'm not that person." The very thing we wanted him to do on the show was not going to happen. We plowed our way through the hour. He tried to help, but we wound up having a serious conversation with a man that the public knew only as a funny fellow. That hour lasted about 300 minutes.

Things were different with Charles O. Finley, the new owner of the Kansas City Athletics, who lived in Chicago. He came on strong. "This is a wonderful town," he told us. "I've called my wife and told her, Let's get ready to move to Kansas City. This is it!" On and on he went. When the show was over, we emerged onto the sidewalk along Baltimore with Finley and the sports editor of *The Kansas City Star*, Ernie Mehl, just ahead of us. We watched them turn the corner at 12th Street.

"What did you think of that guy?" I asked Jean, and she responded, "He's a phony baloney." She was right. He never moved to Kansas City — but he did move the team to California.

In February 1962, on the day John Glenn made his first flight into space, our guest was Charlton Heston. We planned to tape an interview with him to be played the next day. Naturally, there was apprehension about Glenn's re-entry into the atmosphere, and Heston asked to delay the taping of the show so that we could watch on television. When Glenn was safely back, Heston, thrilled with the success of the flight, bought drinks for the house. We did the taping and he had a chance to plug his new movie, "El Cid."

Many years later, after Heston had stirred controversy with his stand on firearms, he came to the studios of KCUR for another talk show. KCUR, a public radio station, was about to begin its fund drive and station manager Patty Cahill thought we might prevail on Heston to record a promotion for it. She prepared two. In one, he was to acknowledge being a member of the National Rifle Association and also being a right winger and to urge listeners nevertheless to contribute. Heston pushed that one aside, saying "Yes, I'm a member of the NRA, but I'm not a right-winger."

However, he was happy to read the second one — he gave it three readings, each better than the last. Adopting his most god-like voice, the one used in the movies, Heston said: "I command you to support public radio and the Walt Bodine Show."

The Rev. Norman Vincent Peale, author of *The Power of Positive Thinking,* came on our show and got angry when I asked him whether he could be considered a "theological Little Mary Sunshine." Before I knew it he replied, "Hell, no!"

"Conversation" went on the road one year to Aspen, Colorado, where the International Design Conference was taking place. World-renowned thinkers had gathered there in the mountains, giving us a wealth of possible programs. We visited with one of the heroes of our time — not a John Glenn or a Scott Carpenter, but a hero of the laboratory, Dr. Jonas Salk. Discussing his groundbreaking research into polio, he told about arranging various ingredients in various ways, searching for the right combination. Had he ever wanted to leave one line of inquiry on a whim, just to try something new?

"It's funny you ask," he said, and recounted how he was on his boat one weekend during his search for ways to defeat the polio virus. He got a hunch that day, and switched direction when he returned to his investigations; the change led to a breakthrough in his research. With that, our chat turned to the subject of creativity. There we were in Aspen, surrounded by artists, designers, musicians — creative people of all kinds. I wondered whether the world of science, where hard facts were added up and mathematics and physical laws wouldn't seem to leave a lot of mental elbow room, had room for what we call creativity. Salk believed it did.

I mentioned a theory I had read, that ideas develop in the subconscious mind and, when they are ready, pop up like pieces of toast in a toaster. Beguiling as that theory was, I was sure it was too simple. To my surprise, Salk agreed with it in a general way. He said his best ideas often came when he had turned his mind from his work, or when he was doing quiet, ordinary things.

Daring to speculate on that with a great scientist I said, "Do you think it possible that someday someone will actually uncover the secret of creativity?"

Salk smiled — and he had a quiet smile that he dispensed economically.

"No," he said. "It's magic."

It was frustrating to encounter people who were normally eloquent on the podium, but couldn't handle a conversation on the radio — particularly people who shaped ideas in our society. Dr. Karl Menninger fit that category. The mere sight of a microphone made him freeze. Twice, I succeeded in getting him to try. If he didn't like it we could stop, I promised, because we were taping. He'd take the mike, start to talk, sputter a little and say, "No, I can't do it."

In Aspen, Menninger was one of the speakers at the Design Conference. I reached him, and he turned me down, but I persisted: "Dr. Menninger, we're a long ways from home. Let's have lunch tomorrow. I'll have a small microphone and we can just talk casually. If you don't like it we can just throw it away." Finally, he said, "OK, we'll have lunch anyway."

My partner, Jean Glenn, and our engineer, Ed Shepherd, and I went to the restaurant ahead of time and arranged everything with the management. Ed placed the tape recorder on a chair where he hoped it would be out of sight and propped the microphone by the salt shaker on the table. During lunch we chatted good-naturedly and I said, "Let's talk for a moment about your book *The Crime of Punishment*." I asked a few questions, everything was going well and I thought we had made it over the

127

hump. Then I noticed that Menninger's eyes had found the tape recorder. He interrupted himself in the middle of a sentence and said, "Oh, shut that damn thing off." We turned it off, but I urged him on, pointing out that he had spoken before thousands of people at the conference. I also reminded him that he had the final word on whether the recording would be used on the air.

"If I've got the final word," the famous psychiatrist said, "the word is that I don't want to do it."

I will always regret that I didn't get that remarkable man on tape.

One day Nathan Leopold appeared on "Conversation." In 1924, Leopold and a friend, Richard Loeb, kidnaped and killed a boy named Bobby Franks in Chicago. Leopold and Loeb were well-to-do college students who had tried to commit the perfect crime. Their case became one of the most celebrated of the 1920s and their names were notorious. Loeb was slain in prison in the 1930s. Leopold eventually was paroled after he had reached his 50s. He was on his way to Puerto Rico where he would study birds, teach math and work as an X-ray technician at a church-operated hospital. On our show Leopold, once considered such a monster, seemed like a religious man bent on serving society. You'd never have suspected he was a convicted murderer.

Bobby Kennedy appeared for a special breakfast session of "Conversation." He was passing through Kansas City on his way to California, advancing the candidacy of his brother, John, for president. Bobby had bright, blue eyes and a ready smile. When he was serious he became very serious, but he also had a great sense of humor.

Talk-show hosts learn to try to size up guests beforehand by such things as their handshake. Shaking hands with Bobby Kennedy, I was surprised to find that he was barely taller than I, and his hand was even smaller than mine.

Even as "Conversation" was flourishing, Bill Leeds and I started a weekly prime-time local talk show on WDAF-TV called "Insight." We patterned it on a British show, whose creator told us that American interviews were usually dull because the interviewer spent too much time getting chummy with the guest, forgetting about the audience. On "Insight," Bill and I accomplished a better relationship with the audience by placing a long coffee table on the set. The guests sat at one end. Bill and I sat at the other end, across from each other and about five feet away from the guest. The camera often looked over our shoulders at the guest, so the viewers could feel they were among the questioners. As the word got around about our show, we stopped having to look for guests. The public-relations people were calling us to arrange appearances. Bobby Kennedy was also our guest on "Insight," as were the baseball star Jackie Robinson and Pierre Salinger, press secretary in the Kennedy administration.

Often in the talk-show world, word gets to you that an upcoming guest is a tough interview. Sometimes, that's because he or she has been coached by a movie studio's public-relations department about what to say and what not to say. Certain lines are trotted out to answer all your questions. The hardest is when you hear that someone like that is scheduled on your show at 10 a.m., but two hours beforehand you hear him chatting with a disc jockey, giving the same stock responses that he'll say to you.

One Tuesday night on "Insight," our guest was an undersecretary in the Treasury Department and the topic was to be the balance of payments. We booked him on the show for his status, not his topic, but we did our research nevertheless. It was in vain. The man was simply dull, making little attempt to explain things. We could sense the dials of all those sets out there clicking to other stations — and the ratings falling through the floor.

I had been up late the night before, and as our guest began another long-winded answer I nodded off to sleep, live on television. Fortunately, the director was a friend. Seeing me falling asleep on Camera Two, he stayed with the other cameras. Meanwhile, he cut off my mike and instructed one of the stagehands to crawl out on the set, below eye level. The stagehand tugged at my coat, which roused me. I looked down and saw the stagehand carefully forming words with his lips: "You were sleeping." We still had about 10 minutes to go and Bill Leeds was looking at me for the next question. As the guest wound down he began to look at me, too, but thankfully the camera didn't shift to me. The control room had thought of the same thing I had: How could I ask a question when I didn't even know how long I'd been asleep? I had no idea what had transpired during my absence. Somehow, Bill came up with another question and the guest took off on another long, dreary answer.

One of our biggest coups was landing Pierre Salinger. It was an entertaining hour, which we taped one afternoon to run the next day, but one response was emblematic of that long-ago era when a president's pecadilloes were masked better than they are today. Given President Kennedy's general popularity, I asked Salinger whether he had any faults, to which the press secretary replied, "Yes he does; he steals pens." When an aide took something to Kennedy for his signature, Salinger said, the president would sign and stick the pen in his pocket — no matter how much the pen cost. Salinger said he was considering converting his entire supply to inexpensive Bic pens.

That night we appeared with Salinger at the Griddle Club, hosted by the Kansas City Press Club. As we said goodbye, I had no idea I would be seeing him again soon. About 2:30 a.m. an engineer woke me up at home, sounding unhappy, and said, "Hey, you know that thing you shot with Salinger? It was a bad tape. See if you could get him to shoot it again."

"You must be kidding," I replied. He wasn't. I called Salinger at that wee hour of the morning and happily he agreed to do the show again, if we could make it very early. We shot it at 7 a.m. Afterward, Salinger called the airline, persuaded it to hold his flight, hopped into a cab and waved goodbye.

The legendary comedian Joe E. Lewis told us about his experience working for mob-operated nightclubs in Chicago. Once, a thug grabbed him just as he was going to go on stage and said, "All right, comedian, get out there and be funny."

I'll always remember Martin Luther King as a guest who seemed ill at ease. When he joined us it was not long after his famous incarceration in the jail in Birmingham for his protests against segregation. He answered our questions well, but wasn't overly talkative. He had had many encounters with the press, but perhaps little experience on an interview show in a studio.

Later, we had his wife, Coretta King, on a WDAF radio show. Among the fascinating things she told us was that she had been moved by a call from Jackie Kennedy at the time her husband was in the Birmingham jail. Mrs. Kennedy said to Mrs. King: "You know, you and I are in the same boat. We never know when our husbands go out the door whether we will ever see them alive again." Within a span of five years, both women would become widows.

When the irascible Thomas Hart Benton appeared as a guest on "Insight," he inevitably made good copy for the press the next day. Once I asked him what he thought about contemporary Russian art. His response: "Russian art is almost as bad as American advertising art and that is bad enough." That made it into *Time* magazine.

Once, Randall Jessee and his wife, Fern, and Bernie, my wife, and I were invited to the Bentons' house for a spaghetti dinner prepared by a fine Italian hand, Rita Benton. While the women visited in the kitchen, Benton invited us down to the basement to see his new furnace. Randall and I looked at each other quizzically, because the artist didn't seem to be the sort of man interested in home heating equipment. We found that he wasn't. The furnace, it turned out, made a fine hiding place for a fifth of Missouri bourbon. Benton reached on top of the furnace, brought down the bottle and passed it around. Each of us took a swig and passed it to the next person, each time exhaling in manly fashion. As we stood there I noticed what appeared to be one of his most famous works, "Persephone," leaning against the basement wall.

"Tom," I asked, "is that what I think it is? Is that the original 'Persephone'?"

"Yeah."

"We have a coffee-table art book that devotes an entire page in color to that painting and here it is leaning against your basement wall. Is this a problem?"

"Nope," Benton said, "and it's going to stay there until Rita gets what she thinks it's worth."

As I recall, Rita was hoping at the time to get something like $35,000 for the painting. Both the Bentons parted this life before they saw that piece make its way into the Nelson. The museum paid millions for it.

One of my favorite interview subjects was Dean Acheson, the embattled but excellent secretary of state under Harry S. Truman. When Acheson appeared on "Insight," a political furor was building over what was called "secret diplomacy." What did Acheson think?

"Mr. Bodine, there is no diplomacy except secret diplomacy," he said. "What they are talking about — summit conferences and the like — would be better described as showboating for publicity. The real diplomacy *is* in secret."

The State Department, he said, monitors constantly the public statements of foreign leaders. "One day they may notice that on some issue where the other side has been hardnosed they seem to be indicating a little willingness to talk about it," Acheson said. "That's all it takes. Next thing, we're on the phone talking to the foreign minister of Russia, for example, and letting him know that we noted the change and asking him whether we should get together to talk it over. A lot of things are settled that way."

The upshot was that back channels were the main channels for getting things done in world affairs.

When I went to work at WDAF radio and then WDAF television, *The Kansas City Star* owned both. In the wake of an antitrust suit, the newspaper had to sell both in 1958. The stations were sold again in 1960. As general manager, Bill Bates managed not only to hold things together but also to improve the stations through those three ownerships. He made money for the owners, kept professional standards high and held the respect of just about everyone.

Bates was one of the most remarkable people I knew at WDAF. We had started together in the business as announcers right after World War II. My career led to the newsroom and the performing side, while Bill aspired to management. With his ability and knowledge he rose quickly. He became station manager of WDAF-TV in 1953 and general manager in 1958. He also had a great voice. Whenever the network decided to originate a show in Kansas City,

Bill was picked to do the commercials. During his radio career, he handled Edgar Bergen and Charlie McCarthy, Carmen Caballero, Fred Waring and many other NBC programs.

Bill kept an eye peeled for trends in society. The postwar Baby Boom meant thousands of young women, many of them college-educated and once interested in careers, got married instead and spent their time raising children. In popular publications of the time, they were referred to collectively as "the trapped housewife." Bill took note of these young women, who clearly felt left out of the big changes in our country. He gave our station a slogan aimed at young women: "WDAF-TV — Your Window on the World."

He was still in charge of the station in late 1963 when the Taft Broadcasting Company of Ohio agreed to buy both the radio and television stations. In spring 1964, after winning Federal Communications Commission approval, Taft took over the management. One of our first encounters with the owners came when department heads were called to a meeting and told not to worry about changes. At that very moment, other management people were meeting with Bill Bates and moving him out of the WDAF general manager's job.

I knew then that if Bates was being treated like this, with his high professional standards and excellent financial performance, there wouldn't be much hope for the rest of us. We were hearing from people at other stations that had been purchased by Taft, telling us to look out because lots of heads probably would roll. I braced myself for big changes and when they came, they were even bigger than I expected.

One affected the newsroom that I headed. WDAF-TV and radio had long enjoyed bureau status with NBC news. Although we weren't an actual news bureau of NBC, the network was confident enough of our reporters and photographers to have us handle stories in our region as if we were network staff. We were proud of that, and when Nick Bolton, one of the new Taft managers, dropped into the newsroom one day, he saw a clipboard on the wall and asked me what it was. I explained to him our close relationship with the network and how we originated a lot of stories for NBC television and radio, rotating them among the staff. Bolton didn't seem impressed with any of that, and he wanted to know who paid our reporters for that work. I told him they were paid by the network at its standard rate for correspondents.

"Well, what do we get out of it?" he asked.

Stunned, I said it was a distinction for a station to be that close to the network and to be trusted that much. Also, the exposure was a good thing for the city.

We should add a surcharge for the station, Bolton replied. At that moment I knew our relationship with the network would be diminished. It was also at that moment that I knew Taft Broadcasting was not where I was going to fit.

Other changes came quickly. I had played an important role in the conversion of WDAF radio to a news-talk format, which we were doing in increments. When Taft took over, we were running news and talk shows from morning drive time through early afternoon. Among them was "Conversation," which enjoyed a good audience. I was startled when Bolton informed me that

"Conversation" would move to 10:30 at night.

It has been said that freedom of the press is freedom for people who happen to own a press. The same principle applies to those who own a radio or television station. When Taft took charge, I wondered how it would use that freedom. It didn't take long to find out. In Barry Goldwater's campaign against Lyndon Johnson for president in 1964, I saw for the first time in my career corporate ownership of a station dictate how the news was gathered and reported. From headquarters in Cincinnati, the head of the company, Hub Taft, sent instructions by teletype for Taft stations to refrain from running any public-opinion polls in the presidential race. The traditionally conservative Taft organization supported Goldwater, but Goldwater trailed in most of the polls. Polls in any presidential campaign are big news and are typically reported with commentaries by news media throughout the country. Now all Taft stations were to pretend that they didn't exist? I put the dispatch from headquarters in a file in my desk, and WDAF went on covering the news as it happened, including the polls.

We had dispatched Bill Leeds, our top reporter, to join the press covering Barry Goldwater. We thought that this was a generous contribution to the campaign. Yet Taft Broadcasting headquarters in Ohio telephoned WDAF's general manager, complaining that Leeds was reporting what Goldwater said instead of what was written in the prepared text of his speech. Goldwater had a habit of digressing from the text and often that generated news. When it happened, Leeds would cover the digressions, just as most in the press corps did. Soon, Taft headquarters was demanding Leeds be taken off the Goldwater campaign. He was assigned to cover Lyndon Johnson, and Taft put one of its own men on Goldwater. The new reporter did what he was asked, giving glowing accounts of how a smiling Goldwater was winning over the crowds. Now, we all knew that a single phone call from Cincinnati could alter our careers. In broadcasting, security is precious because there is damned so little of it.

In 1965 I resigned from WDAF mainly because of differences with the Taft Broadcasting Company. I posted a memo in the coffee room. It contained a brief paragraph saying that sometimes you come to the point where you have to march to the beat of a different drummer. It saddened me to leave Signal Hill, where our organization had spent so many years building a high-quality television and radio operation.

Meanwhile, my long, slow descent toward blindness had begun. I had noticed for a while that it was becoming harder to take a strip of film from a photographer, hold it up to the light and decide what we would include in a story. I realized that it would be difficult to be a news director or anchor on television, and decided that it would be better to jump back into radio. I went from eye doctor to eye doctor and finally got a confirmed diagnosis. My symptoms showed the onset of retinitis pigmentosa, a degenerative disease of the eyes. In some cases, vision is lost within months. In others, the loss takes years. I was one of the lucky ones.

Just as I was looking for a new job, WHB radio was ready for a change in the host of its venerable "Nightbeat" talk show. I ran into a WHB executive, Don Loughnane, at dinner in one of the restaurants on an upper story of Commerce Tower. I told him that I was ready to leave Taft. The next day he called and said WHB was interested in me. I met with some top executives and they described the changes they wanted to make in "Nightbeat." We arrived at a salary, and I was on board.

INTERLUDE

Face to face with viewers

Early in the television game I remember walking downtown when a man stepped over and almost blocked my path.

"Are you him?" he said, as I stared at him. "Excuse me, I never saw any of you fellows out of the box before."

*   *   *

One day I was going up the escalator at Commerce Tower and a woman on the way down began to look at me and point.

"Am I unzipped or what?" I wondered.

As she got close she said, "Are you him?"

"I guess so."

She reached out and grabbed my arm as she continued to go down and I continued to go up. I finally had to give a mighty pull to release myself from her clutches.

*   *   *

Some people see you and think that they know you from somewhere. If they stop you to talk, you know that this is likely to be an ill-fated encounter. They're saying: "Well, how are you? Haven't seen you lately. How's the family?" After they walk on, it will hit them that they don't actually know you — you're just a guy from television.

*   *   *

There are some hazards when you're out in public. There's the guy who comes up to you and says: "Say, I watch your show all the time. Let me tell you about what I'm doing…. I think it would make a very good talk show. In fact, some of my friends have said that I ought to call you and tell you that I ought to be on the show." From that moment on, you seal your lips, listen, act pleasant, and nod a little because anything you say will create 10 minutes of response. When he finally stops long enough, I cut in to say, "I'm glad to have heard about that and it was very good to meet you." I shake hands and make a point of returning to what I was doing before he approached.

That will not always stop the self-promoter who comes up to you in a restaurant. He may make a second run on your table. If he does, he has ruled himself out as a potential talk-show guest. One such character, after two encounters at the table, was waiting by the front door to give me his final push, "Yes, I'd sure like to be on that show." I headed for the car, fearing if I didn't hurry he'd be trying to talk through the car window.

*   *   *

After a while you learn how to protect yourself from some things. Let's say you're out for dinner with a friend and you're in a booth at a nice restaurant. My tactic is to sit at the edge of the booth, leaving the empty space by the wall and not where it can invite someone to sit down. Otherwise, even if you're having a serious conversation someone will come up and say, "Gee, I've been listening to you for years," sit down and want to have a nice long talk. That happened once when I was negotiating a contract for a new job. Just as we were getting to the difficult part, the waiter came along.

"You need anything else?" he asked. "It's a fine day out isn't it? Don't you need some more coffee?"

"No," I finally said. "We don't want anything except to finish our conversation here."

*   *   *

Some people on television made a lasting impression on the public but not a deep one. Randall Jessee was Kansas City's first and for several years only local TV anchorman and every night he said, "This is Randall Jessee with the news" and "This is Randall Jessee at the end and good night." Nevertheless, about one in five letters came addressed to Jesse Randall.

*   *   ʌ

Half a dozen years after stepping away as early anchor on Channel 4 news, I regularly ran into people who'd say, "I watch you on the news all the time — saw you on the 6 o'clock news last night."

Then there are the people who will stop and praise you for being an excellent sportscaster, telling you they wouldn't listen to anyone else. Since the first week of my career, I've never been a sportscaster and never wanted to be.

*   *   *

From time to time you'll meet someone on the street who was once your guest on a show. I have been involved in radio and television talk shows for more than 40 years. He or she will say: "Remember

me? I was on your show about four years ago." You
make some lame comment like, "So many people
come and go on the show, it gets hard to remember
anybody." He may even tell you his topic but even if
you don't recall it, you always give him the benefit of
the doubt, smile and go your merry way.

*   *   *

People developed personal attachments to those
they saw on the air and would call them. At WDAF
my desk and Randall Jessee's faced each other, so we
couldn't help see and hear some of what went on the
other side. One night a little old lady from Butler,
Missouri, came to the station and asked to see
Randall. Many in this business would have said,
"Not now," but Randall said, "Send her on up." She
told him that she was alone in the world and doctors
had told her that she would need an operation to
save her life. Even after gathering all her money she
was $100 short of what it would take.

I overheard this story and thought, "Oh,
brother, this is a con routine of some kind."

But Randall was a good-hearted man. He
listened carefully to her, reached in his pocket and
came out with a C-note for her.

"I knew I could depend on you Mr. Jessee," she
said. "Most of my folks are gone now. But I thought,

he's a nice man and I see him every night. I know he will be good to me."

It turned out that her story was real. A few weeks later she came back and said, "Mr. Jessee, I just want to thank you. I had the operation and I'm a lot better."

Randall is a nicer man than I am, I thought afterward. He didn't question her need.

Presidents

Lyndon Johnson

One day in 1960 I was co-hosting "Conversation" on WDAF with Jean Glenn and preparing to interview a well-known local figure, Nathan Stark, when Harry S. Truman and Lyndon B. Johnson, then a U.S. senator, came through the door of Bretton's. Johnson had recently been nominated for vice president of the United States. The waiter ushered the two back to an out-of-the-way booth and seated them. I turned to my guest and said, "If I could get Senator Johnson over, would you mind putting off our interview?" He agreed. So I worked up my courage and went back to their booth and addressed Truman:

"We're doing a live radio show in the front of Bretton's in a few minutes and wondered whether it might be all right with you if Senator Johnson could appear as our guest."

Johnson reacted immediately, saying, "Well, I'm here to see President Truman. I'm a guest of President Truman...." Before he could go any further, Truman said to him, "Lyndon, you're running for vice president of the United States, and if one of these fellows wants to stick a microphone in your face, you talk into it. I'll wait for you."

We adjourned to the front table, Johnson sitting just to my right and Jean Glenn across the table. The possibilities were interesting, partly because of the release in 1959 of Allen Drury's novel of American politics, *Advise and Consent*. It was widely believed that one character in the book — a wheeling, dealing Senate majority leader — was modeled after Johnson. Had the senator read *Advise and Consent*, I asked, and was he aware that the majority leader in the book seemed a great deal like him? Johnson's eyebrows furrowed.

"Mr. Bodine," he began, "Mr. Allen Drury is a very good friend of mine and he told me personally, as a matter of fact, that the Senate majority leader was not me. And that it's a work of fiction." We continued the interview a little while before I returned to the book.

"Don't you think there were some very striking resemblances between the Senate majority leader in *Advise and Consent* and you?"

Johnson replied, "Mr. Bodine, I want you to look on the third page of this book and you'll find a paragraph that says, 'Any resemblance to characters living or dead is purely coincidental.' "

We resumed the conversation and he gave us some boilerplate that went something like this: "I always feel I improve myself when I come to Jackson County. And I always like to be on… (he leaned around to see the call letters)… WDAF."

I risked it one more time: "Senator Johnson, I just can't get over the haunting feeling that that's you in this novel."

At that point, his giant hand came down on my not too-large forearm and gave it a mighty squeeze. Were those my bones crunching?

"If it's all right with you, Mr. Bodine, I think we've talked about that enough. Let's talk about something else."

I agreed.

*   *   *

In 1965 Johnson, by then president, and Vice President Hubert Humphrey came to town to sign Medicare into law. A motorcade escorted them from Municipal airport to the Truman Library in Independence where the historic event was to take place. Truman had been the first president to

propose such a health-care bill. The motorcade
moved fast, and police swarmed over every tall
building along the route. It was the first time the
president and vice president had been in the same
motorcade since the assassination of President
Kennedy in Dallas.

When the signing ceremony was over, the
motorcade roared back to the airport, where a crowd
of people waited. The press was allowed inside the
fence. Air Force One and Air Force Two were both
there. Johnson got out of the car, walked to the
plane, shook hands with several people, went up the
stairs, turned, gave a final wave, and stepped into the
plane. The door came shut. I looked around and
noticed that the vice president was standing nearby,
waiting, as it turned out, for Air Force One to depart
before his plane could leave. Air Force One wheeled
to the right, heading for the runway. As it did, it
blew sand and dirt in the faces of all of us standing
there. We ducked underneath the rolling stairs that
had just been pulled away from the plane. I glanced
across to see Hubert Humphrey there with us,
huddled under the stairs, waiting for all that dust
and sand to stop so that we could come back out.
Face to face with Humphrey, I could read it in his
demeanor: "This is how it is as vice president of the
United States."

Later, with considerably less fanfare, Humphrey

stepped aboard Air Force Two, told us goodbye and left. I had the feeling that Hubert Humphrey was thinking about the insignificance of his role as he flew back to the capital. It was well known that there wasn't a tremendous lot of love lost between Johnson and Humphrey. At the same time, I couldn't help thinking about the words of a long-ago vice president who said the position was the most insignificant ever conceived by the mind of man.

C H A P T E R   V I

WHB - ''Nightbeat'' - A Lion in the Studio -
On Top of the World - Enter the Consultant - ''Town Hall'' -
Startup TV Station - Working Here, Working There

My talk shows have run the gamut. "Nightbeat," the late-night show on WHB, had a lot in common with a grocery tabloid. The subjects ranged from mind-reading to faith-healing to UFO sightings. "Nightbeat" began at 10 p.m. and ended at 1 a.m. In those three hours, I am certain, the I.Q. of the audience gradually shrank.

My engineer was Bob Cleary, a native of Arkansas. Each night I greeted him with, "How are you, Bob?" Each night he answered, "Fine as frog's hair!"

Bob was ever vigilant. If it had been a long day for me, I was inclined to let a caller ramble on. I'd begin thinking about something else and sometimes good sense went out the window. On one such night, when my mind had drifted, I came back to reality with a regular caller, a railroad engineer, who was saying:

"Well, what do you think? Do you think that would work?"

I had no idea what he was talking about, but decided to chance it and said, "Yeah, sure."

"Really, do you think it would?"

"Yeah," I said quickly, just as we were ending the show. "…And that winds up tonight's 'Nightbeat.' See you tomorrow."

When it was over Bob Cleary came in and said: "Do you know that last guy that called? You know when he said, 'What do you think?' and you said, 'Sure'? You know what he asked you?"

"No," I said, "What happened? What did I agree to?"

"He asked you if you thought as he did that it would be a good idea for Kansas City to save money by taking the police helicopters and flying them upside down and very low over Loose Park so that the propellers could cut the grass and you wouldn't have to have all of those lawnmowers."

When something like that happens, you put on your coat and hat and drive out into the night, hoping the streets are filled with non-listeners.

Sometimes the characters in the neighborhood around the station could be more interesting than the callers. The WHB studios were in the 11th-floor penthouse atop the declining Pickwick Hotel. One of my favorite people there was Manny, the head bellhop. I don't know how Manny got to Kansas City from Chicago or why, but he seemed to know many mobsters. Once, he told me a hit-man from Detroit had just checked in and that within a few days someone would be bumped off.

One summer evening I was coming out from doing the show and Manny was standing outside having a smoke. At the corner was a pale-faced man in a black cape and thick glasses.

"What have we here?" I wondered out loud.

"He's probably a ribbon clerk from Wichita," Manny said, "who lives for coming up here and looking scary."

One mid-afternoon, I went in to do some extra work, and then headed downstairs for an early dinner at the coffee shop. In those days, there were several women soliciting business at the Pickwick — "hot and cold running call girls," as one of the bellhops said. One of them slid in beside me at the counter and ordered a cup of coffee. We chatted as I dined on roast beef on toast.

"These afternoon tricks are killing me," she said, "but you can turn $100 on one good trick. I just want to get a quick cup of coffee and hurry home because I've got to make cupcakes for the PTA." With that, she slid off the stool, paid her check and left. You learn a lot about life in a place like that.

One night on "Nightbeat" the topic was "Exotic Pets in the City." Callers brought up pet chipmunks and monkeys, but I didn't expect the man who called and said, "I have a lion."

"A real lion?" I said, "like on the front of an MGM picture?"

"Yes, just like that," the man replied.

"How far away do you live?"

He said he lived in an apartment on Roanoke Road.

"Now this is getting to be too much for me, pal," I said. "I can't believe that you can be living in an apartment on Roanoke and have a lion for a pet. Where does he sleep?"

"He sleeps in the bathtub. Kind of cools him off, I guess."

"OK, I think I'm being conned, but in case I'm not, bring that lion down here."

I dismissed the matter and went on to a woman who said she had twin canaries with red feathers. As I was talking I could look straight up the hall to a glass door where a receptionist sat during the day. The door was locked at night, but you could see people

153

getting off the elevator. Manny, the doorman, who had a key to the door, got off the elevator and came down the hall with a man leading a full-grown lion.

He came in and I said, "Well, I see you really do have a lion." As I was talking, the lion began moving around and sniffing at the calves of my legs. Apparently, I was not Grade A meat because he turned away, but not before my voice had gone up about three octaves. I told the animal's owner to take his pet to the other end of the studio, where there was a big metal stanchion, the kind of post used to zone people off at the movies. The lion owner took him down and fastened the lion's collar to the stanchion. The lion settled down beside it. The stanchion was heavy, so I thought, "That takes care of that" and relaxed.

As we continued to talk the lion owner revealed that he was not a lion expert. In fact, he had owned the lion only a couple of weeks. I was in there with a wild beast and a guy who didn't really know much about how to manage it. Then I heard the stanchion fall over. The lion was dragging it behind him as he strolled over for another sniff of the backs of my legs.

"It was wonderful of you to come," I told the animal's owner. "We've now got some other things to do so I want to bid you goodnight." He and his big pet left, but I thought about the folks who typically sat around the lobby of the Pickwick after having a few cocktails. What kind of commotion happened when that man and his pet stepped off the elevator on their way out?

A man who called himself Ahman Karr called me from a place called Echo Valley near Tonganoxie, Kansas, to say how much he and his friends enjoyed listening to "Nightbeat." I thanked him.

"We were hoping next Sunday you could come to our open house at Echo Valley to meet all of the fans of your show," he said.

"Well, possibly I could do that. Where is this?"

"It's near Tonganoxie but it's not in the city limits." I asked what they did there and he said, "Well, we are nature-lovers and children of the sun."

Finally it dawned on me: this guy was talking about a nudist camp. If I paid a visit, would I have to adopt their lifestyle?

"Oh, no. Come right on."

I didn't go and I will never know.

At 1 a.m., after "Nightbeat" signed off, WHB continued on autopilot. As usual, I was the only one left in the studio and stayed to write my nightly report with the studio door open. In the middle of composing it one night, I saw from the corner of my eye a large man standing in what should have been an empty room, wearing a turban with a knife stuck in his belt. Clearly, he was going to come in and I decided to chance a bold tactic.

"Hold it right there," I said, firmly. "You realize this is a federally authorized operation and no one can come in here who is not either an employee or an invited guest on the show. We don't want to get you in any trouble. Do you want to talk to me?"

"Yeah, I want to talk," he said.

"Just go right down the hall to the announcer's lounge and wait until I finish this report."

He did so, thank God. This man was big enough to be trouble. As soon as he was out of sight, I called downstairs to Manny, the bell captain, to alert the police and send reinforcements. Then I continued to type my report. What an ending I'd have! My man stayed in the announcer's lounge. I was greatly relieved when the glass doors opened and Manny and a couple of cops came down the hall. They brought the man out, walked him up the hall, and took him back to the mental institution he had walked away from earlier in the evening. He had ridden the elevator up to the lobby of our penthouse studio, where the glass entrance doors were locked. Another door, however, led to the roof and he walked out on it and around to a window, which he simply raised and entered. When someone later asked me why the windows weren't locked, I said, "How many people on the 11th floor of anything lock their windows?"

At WHB the signal was directional, strongest to the northeast and southwest. We got mail from listeners in New London, Ontario, and in Big Spring, Texas, but reception in parts of Johnson County was poor. One night I got a call from a gentleman who identified himself as a radioman assigned to the aircraft carrier *Wasp*. Was he visiting in town?

"No. In fact, we're picking up your signal on the aircraft carrier, traveling down toward the tip of South Africa."

We talked for some time about their trip and talked to some of the men aboard. It was being broadcast through speakers all over the ship. That was a thrill for me. It's rare for a signal to bounce that far and be that clear.

Jerry Lewis appeared once on "Nightbeat" and he began entertaining even before he entered the studio. As he came through the Pickwick's revolving door, the doorman told me, he pretended to be caught, stumbled and almost turned himself upside down in one of his patented pratfalls. At these antics, people in the lobby laughed hysterically. However, once the show began upstairs and the calls started coming in, he became snippy. When someone told him how wonderful he was, he'd give a curt, distant and sarcastic reply: "Oh, sure…."

At a a station break I said: "You know, all of these people are saying how much they enjoy you and you are barking back at them. This is the Midwest, not the West Coast. When people say things like that here, they mean it."

He looked stunned for a moment and when we returned to the air he changed his tune. He even agreed to stay longer than his scheduled 30 minutes to make up for it.

Al Capp, creator of Lil' Abner, was wonderful. Someone from out of town tipped me that he could be grouchy before he'd had a drink or two, so we arranged with the hotel bartender to ship drinks up to him every 20 minutes. Capp turned out to be a jovial guest.

I always looked forward to the visits of Jack Swift, who had been a terrific reporter for *The Star's* morning edition, *The Kansas City Times*. Like many journalists of his day, he had been a heavy drinker, but that did not stop him from doing a remarkable job. One night when I worked at *The Star* building for WDAF in the late 1940s, I watched him leave to cover a fire in an apartment building on 10th Street where there had been fatalities and injuries. As the deadline crept closer, Jack Swift returned to the newsroom, cigarette dangling from his lips and looking a little woozy. He sat down in front of the typewriter, groused a bit at the copy boy who stood beside him, took off his coat, lit another cigarette and started to write. As he wrote, he'd come to a fact he needed — the name and age of a victim, for instance — and begin to look through his pockets. The information might turn up on the inside of a matchbook cover. As soon as Swift finished a couple of paragraphs, he pulled them out of the typewriter and gave them to the copy boy, who'd run them to the city desk and run back for the next few. I could imagine the mental process Jack was going through — trying to remember what he had already written and what he still needed to write. But he chain-smoked his way through, made his deadline, and the story was published. From those scraps of paper and cardboard that were his notebook, he wrote a terrific story with dashes of color.

Jack Swift was one of the best talk-show guests we ever had. He was plainspoken. Once on "Nightbeat," a woman called to say: "Mr. Swift, I just don't think it's very nice for you to talk the way you do. The way you spoke to that last caller…."

"Ma'am, I'm not nice," he responded. "I don't even try. This world has too many nice people now. What I try to be is good. We never have enough good people. Kansas City is loaded with nice people."

If Jesus Christ were on earth now, he continued, he probably wouldn't be spending much time with nice folks and do-gooders. He said that Jesus probably would be with the poor, the workers and the outcasts.

Jack Swift became one of my closest friends. When he stopped drinking, he had to go on strict diets because of diabetes. He ended up as director of the National Council on Alcoholism in Kansas City. I'm old enough to have watched many friends be carried away by death, but there are none I miss more than the plainspoken and honorable Jack Swift.

There was always plenty of action around "Nightbeat," but the most dramatic moments came amid the riots of April 1968. They began with a confrontation between black demonstrators and police at City Hall and continued through days of burning and looting. The last thing the city needed, I thought, was for "Nightbeat" to become a soapbox for rabble-rousers and racists. We wondered whether the show should simply go off the air for a week or so. But there was another way: Turn "Nightbeat" into a call-*out* show instead of a call-*in* show. We could call out to the mayor and other political leaders, to clergymen, to civil rights leaders, and to officials of the fire and police departments. We could have a full discussion of the riots on the air without making the situation even more explosive. We were able to talk to people whose comments might help calm things. After about a week we re-opened the lines, let people ventilate and in time things settled down.

In the course of this I met Alvin Brooks. He had been in the streets among the protesters, but in time helped to calm things down. Alvin agreed to come to the station with others who had been caught up in protests. Together we did a few specials. Brooks and others finally could be heard by an establishment that had found it all too easy to ignore them in the past. Since then, Alvin has been a respected voice in all sectors of the city. His career has included a job as a policeman, teacher, city director of human relations, one of the creators of the Ad Hoc Citizens Against Crime and member of the City Council and mayor pro tem. He has also been a very good friend.

While I was doing "Nightbeat" I felt on top of the world. My ratings were high. Then a broadcast consulting company came to town.

One day in 1968 I arrived at work and was told the station manager wanted to see me. After the usual formalities, he told me that the consultants had reviewed the station and suggested it was difficult to serve two audiences — a youth audience during the day with Top 40 music, and a "Nightbeat" audience that skewed toward older adults. The consultants recommended that the station drop "Nightbeat" and replace it with a disc-jockey program. When would the change be made? I asked. The manager told me that that night's show would be the last. He also asked that I not say anything about going off the air, but just to sign off in the usual way. That struck me as a sneaky way out.

I suggested we let people know what was going on, give them a chance to respond and do it with about three weeks of lead time. On the last night, we could thank them for listening. I also told him I was ready to kick up a fuss if we didn't do it like that.

The station manager said that he had to check with the head of the chain, George Armstrong, in Omaha. Within the hour I had a call back from him saying, "George thinks that's a good idea."

After we closed "Nightbeat," WHB decided it wanted to do a public-affairs talk show on Sunday nights and asked me whether I was interested. With a wife and five children, a mortgage and a car payment, I had no other jobs in mind at that time and I agreed. I suggested we call it "Sunday Town Hall."

"Town Hall" lasted six years and drew a respectable audience. It took place on the 22nd floor of the Kansas City Power & Light Building, where WHB had moved its studios from the Pickwick. After a while, there was a big drawback. For some time Mary Nell Moore did a show from 7 to 9 p.m. before "Town Hall." When she left the station I was expected to take over that time, and ended up with a five-hour show. Doing it was a feat, because talk shows run on talk and coffee. When a show goes five hours from 7 to midnight, all those cups of coffee become a problem. Station breaks ran only 30 seconds and we'd be back on the air. The men's restroom was right next door, but the round trip couldn't be made in 30 seconds.

Finally, I got smart. Politicians love to talk and love getting airtime without interruption. So I started bringing in public officials at 10 p.m. I began with an old friend, Charles B. Wheeler Jr. He was then a Jackson County administrative judge, later mayor of Kansas City, and later yet a Missouri state senator. When he came in at 10 p.m. we spoke for a moment or two on the air and then I pushed a note over to him.

"I'm going to leave you now," it said. "I've given you a good question. Please continue to answer it until I get back. Thank you."

As I recall, the first question was: "You've had a good sampling of public life. What's the best and the worst of it?" As he

161

started talking, I was out the door. Relief at last! Charles caught on and I scheduled him once a month. After that I brought in a parade of public officials — mayors, council members, members of Congress and governors from both sides of the state line. Each got the little note at the beginning. If they were any kind of "pol" at all they could fill an hour.

I also invited politicians like George Lehr, who was the first county executive. At that time, the big issue was reassessment of property for taxes, and he was set to talk at length. When we opened up to the audience, however, the biggest issue wasn't what everyone at the courthouse was talking about, but everything from feral dogs wandering in unincorporated areas of the county to chuckholes to wobbly bridges.

From time to time, George Lehr and Charles Wheeler found themselves on opposite sides. One night after a show with Wheeler, George said: "I think I've figured it out. Charlie can one-line you to death. But if the show is long enough he eventually wears out. I'm putting in for a four-hour show with Charlie."

A county sheriff was my only failure in my attempt to get the guests to be long-winded. When I shoved the note across to him, the sheriff looked startled and went silent. I motioned to him to read it again and then asked, "What's the hardest thing about being sheriff and what are the rewards?" I took off, and he began to talk. When I got to the restroom I heard him slowly decreasing his volume and speed. He was beginning to fade out entirely when I made it back to occupy the host's chair. I needed to know my politicians better before I booked them for the 10 o'clock relief hour.

One night we scheduled Wheeler, to be followed by Lehr's successor as county executive, Mike White. Mike always said the worst thing that could happen to him was to follow Charlie Wheeler. As he was driving to appear on the show, he heard a woman call in from the south part of town about problems she was having with dogs running loose. Mike heard Charlie's answer, "Yes, were those Grandview dogs or Kansas City dogs?" Like a trouper, Mike did not turn around and go home.

Earl Butz, secretary of agriculture in the Nixon administration, was famous for saying impolitic things. For a talk-show host he was a handful. Two days before Butz was to tape "Town Hall" on WHB, the Secret Service arrived to do advance work. They wanted to know which elevators he would use, inspected the restroom and asked which stall the secretary would be using, and proceeded into the station. There we settled on where Butz would sit in the studio, making sure his back was not to the door. The agents also wanted to know whether the studio would be locked during the show. They asked me to identify the people behind the glass — one was the producer and the other was the engineer. Having made notes of all of this, they departed. Against this background, Butz came in and we taped the show, talking about a series of agriculture problems, risking the loss of much of the metropolitan audience. At the end of the interview, wanting to elicit a little humor, I said, "As the secretary of agriculture, do you think the rain will hurt the rhubarb?" He responded testily, "There'll always be rhubarbs with programs like this around."

All of this was on tape. We had promoted the Earl Butz interview to be played the following Sunday night. When that night rolled around, we were wending our way through the program leading up to 10 o'clock when the Butz tape was to be played. I glanced over into the control room and was startled to see Will the engineer, normally a calm, affable man, standing there looking through the glass. He was pale-faced and anguished. When we got to the break, he came in and said: "I needed a tape a minute ago and I reached over and got one and put it on the tape eraser and it was the Butz tape. What are we going to do?" The solution was inevitable. We had to admit that we had a technical glitch and that we had indeed lost the Butz tape. This touched a raw nerve with the conspiracy wing of the Republican Party locally. Those faithful thought surely that we media guys had rubbed it out on purpose. Fortunately, the general manager never listened on Sunday nights. In broadcasting, you learn to endure a tempest like that for a week or more. There was lots of mail, calls and other protestations. I just told myself, "This, too, will pass."

Another guest, Sid Willens, a long-time activist lawyer in town, came in with a one-hour show scripted with questions for me to ask and his answers. He was clearly nervous. At one minute before airtime I said, "OK, put on your headset. And by the way, you know everything that is in this paper you wrote here. So let's just talk."

I threw the document in the wastebasket. He looked at me astonished, as if I had committed an act of madness. Nevertheless, we made it through the show and he did very well. In fact, he became so much at ease that later he was a star on KCUR on a series we called "The Hellraisers," in which the public learned Sid's favorite saying, "The price of freedom is eternal publicity."

One night we slated George C. Scott as a guest. Word had come through the talk-show rumor mill that he was a tough one and you'd better hope that he wasn't having anything to drink or he might break up the place. He walked in nicely dressed and wearing rimless glasses, looking a lot like a college professor. His wife, Trish Van Devere, was with him. We sat down and began to talk.

"I'll tell you something," I said. "I'm a great, great fan of yours. I especially loved one particular film that you did."

He said, "Well, I'm a fan of yours."

I said, "Now how could that be?" Scott told me he once taught at Stephens College in Columbia, Missouri, and he often came to Kansas City in those days. At another stage of his life he was driving a truck, passed through Kansas City and heard me on the air. Feeling pleased with myself, we moved off into the matter of his best film. I had a small piece of paper and a pencil for each of us.

"Without anybody watching anybody else," I said, "write the name of the movie — of all the movies that George has done — that is your personal favorite." The three of us put our pieces of paper on the table face down. We talked for a moment longer and then George had the honor of looking at them. The first one, which was mine, said, "Hospital." And the second one, which was Trish Van Devere's also said, "Hospital." Then George turned over his piece of paper and it said, "Hospital." A touching and funny film, all agreed. I seldom see a movie twice, but I saw that one three times.

And if I had anything to tell the talk-show grapevine, it was that it had badly misrepresented George C. Scott.

On the days surrounding my Sunday nights at WHB, I was piecing together a living. Luckily, in October 1969 a new television outlet went on the air, the first locally owned station in the area since *The Star* sold WDAF more than a decade before. Bill Wormington, the general manager and one of a score of local investors, hired me as news director for the new venture — KCIT, Channel 50. My news staff consisted of Mary Loy Brown, who covered days, John Hayes, the evening newscaster, and Steve Bell on nights. I filled in on all those shifts.

The station had no network affiliation, but it had a strategy. As a UHF channel, one of the ultrahigh-frequency bands numbered from the teens through the 80s, KCIT was on a different portion of the TV dial from what most viewers were accustomed to. For a while, we gave away UHF antennas. Our primary pitch, however, was our independence. At that time the three commercial network affiliates in town — WDAF, KCMO and KMBC — had had it their way for years. Given the chance to carry a lucrative one-time show, they'd bump an episode of a regular network show despite objections from the show's loyal viewers. KCIT jumped at the chance to carry those shows. One problem was explaining this succinctly in our promotions. We hired an ad agency, but it didn't coming up with a good answer. In a meeting to discuss the problem, I blurted out, "How about billboards that say, 'See What

You've Been Missing.'" We carried that theme into radio commercials and some print ads. It seemed to work.

Our newscasts were scheduled every half hour. Each lasted a minute and a half, and they opened with, "Now, a TV 50 fastcast." That was a tongue-twister. One of our fill-in announcers, who was not above having a couple of beers waiting his turn, sometimes crashed badly just trying to say the phrase.

KCIT's physical plant was at 2100 Stark in the unincorporated Blue Summit area between Kansas City and Independence. It consisted of a quonset hut containing a makeshift studio, which was attached to a small building containing the control room. Connected to that building was a large trailer with offices for the news and other departments. There wasn't the feeling of permanence you got strolling the halls of Channels 4, 5 or 9. In stormy weather, the hail beating down on our quonset hut was guaranteed to drown out the newscaster's voice and leave the audience wondering whether the station was under machine-gun attack.

Because of a string of technical problems, including power outages, we had trouble staying on the air. When a breakdown occurred in the middle of our 8 o'clock movie, viewers called, screaming. John Hayes created his own formula for answering those complaints. He'd would make his voice sound as if it were an answering machine: "We are sorry for this interruption of service to KCIT-TV. We are working right now to fix this technical problem and should be back on the air shortly." He did a good job imitating a machine, though at the end of the message some callers still said, "Thank you." Whenever an unusually "pretty" voice came on and said, "Thank you" John would say, "That's quite all right, my dear; call again," and hang up.

KCIT had an unusually tall tower, and ice built up on it in winter. When a warm day arrived, chunks of ice dropped off. If the wind was blowing north, the ice fell on a Blue Summit residential neighborhood. One night, as I was sitting at my window writing the newscast, I heard a lot of noise. People were standing outside the studio, shaking their fists and shouting. I opened the door.

"What's up?" I asked.

"Your damned transmitter is bombing our houses," they cried. One man who lived in a trailer home had barely missed being struck by a large chunk of ice that crashed through his roof. I was relieved to be merely the news director. The station manager, I told them, would be there by 9:30 the next morning and I would let him know how they felt.

There were problems aplenty. Nothing shatters your confidence quite like discovering that the cameraman and all the people in the studio are laughing at you while you're on camera. You can't hear the laughter, but you can see it. "What's happened?" you think, "What have I done wrong?" Once we were using a rear-screen projector color-coded to yellow. I stood in front of a yellow background wearing a yellow shirt and tie. No one had told me that you shouldn't wear clothing the same color as the background.

My line was, "Remember: Tonight, 'Stagecoach West' will be the evening feature film beginning at 8 o'clock." They shot me against a scene from the movie showing the stagecoach coming down a hill. It was supposed to disappear when it came to me, but upon reaching my yellow shirt the little stagecoach with its team of horses went rolling across my chest, disappearing perhaps in my inside pocket, only to emerge from my left shoulder a second later.

Looking at the tape, the producer said, "That's all right, let's use it." It made for a little conversation around town — which that station dearly needed.

Before long, KCIT ran into financial difficulties. You knew things were tough when, on payday, employees jumped into their cars to take their paychecks to the rural Missouri bank where the station had its account. In mid-1971 KCIT went under.

The day the station died, the program director, Bill Ladesh, an old hand in the business, had to do the necessary things. As curious executives at other stations around town watched on their own sets, he read on the air a message from the Federal Communications Commission and played the national anthem. Ladesh added his own special touch — the famous Warner Brothers cartoon finale, "That's all, folks!"

For those of us who worked there, the closing created an eerie feeling. We were used to the routines of broadcasting and now none of that mattered. Screens all over the station went dark. Here and there, a knot of people stood and talked. Others loaded their lunch boxes and headed for the parking lot. Some of them looked back, and some didn't.

Even before the end, KCIT faced competition from another locally owned independent, a better-financed one. KBMA — owned by a company headed by the president of Kansas City's Business Men's Assurance Company — went on the air in early autumn 1970 on channel 41. KBMA's manager was Bob Wormington, the twin brother of Bill Wormington, who managed KCIT. For a year or two I worked at various posts at KBMA, producing a special here and there, doing public-service interviews and developing a longstanding relationship in the production of shows with Rob Forsythe, now one of Kansas City's leading producers of commercials. Rob and I teamed up on an eclectic once-a-month show called "Bodine's Beat."

Rob has seen a lot of things in the viewfinder of his camera, but there's one he says he will always remember from that show. He was shooting a scene with me inside a van. Rob was seated next to the driver, leaning around with his camera pointed at me. I was in the back seat behind a small desk, talking away. Suddenly, the van swerved.

"One moment I was looking at you talking." Rob recalled, "and the next minute I was looking at the soles of your shoes."

I'm notorious for not paying a lot of attention to shoes. Jimmy, the morning doorman at the apartment where I live, checks me out now and then as I come down the stairs and occasionally makes a polite, but indirect point: "Hm-m-m-m, one brown shoe, one black shoe. Are they wearing them that way?"

KBMA also gave me the chance to work in a Phil Donahue-style setting, beginning with an interview and continuing in the aisles, taking questions and comments from an audience of 30 to 40 people. The guest interviews went well, but I never became comfortable walking up and down the aisles. You can be interviewing someone on the left side of the aisle and, seeing no one nearby who's ready to talk, swing around to the right side and hope someone wants to contribute. In desperation sometimes I stuck a microphone in front of anyone who simply looked at me in a non-threatening manner.

I kept other irons in the fire and was always looking for opportunities. Once I met a man in a restaurant to discuss a job I was considering. We arrived a little late for our reservations, so we had to wait for our table in the bar. He ordered a Bloody Mary that was not made to his satisfaction. He told the bartender how it should be made. When he received the second one he complained. That continued into the restaurant. He was abusive to the server and I was embarrassed to be with him. By the time lunch was over, I knew I had no interest in that job even though it paid well. What would it be like to work for somebody whose hobby it was to pick at people all the time? How long would I last in such a place?

I told him I appreciated the offer, but I was going to pass for now. As he headed back to his office I felt a pang of sympathy for the people who worked for him.

Once I was working on a public-service interview wearing an earpiece through which I was supposed to hear things such as "You have three and one-half minutes to go," and then, "Thirty seconds! Wrap it up." That day, the wires became crossed and my messages came from a director down the hall who was taping a different show. Naturally, nothing coming from my earpiece made sense. Somehow, I found my way to the end of the show. Yet again in my career, I felt the meaning of "flop sweat," which is as much reality as it is a figure of speech. When something like that is over, you realize you're wet from head to toe.

From 1974 to 1979 I was regional director of the National Conference of Christians and Jews, an organization combating prejudice.

I also worked one year in the Fremerman-Papin advertising agency. There I learned that the advertising business was not quite what I expected from my previous vantage point as a newscaster. I thought ad people walked on thick rugs, hung fake Picassos on the wall and ran up and down halls saying, "Chief, I've got a great idea." They were more serious than that, it turned out. Advertising people not only had to be creative, but also careful about detail. It was hard work and a perilous way to make a living. An agency could be riding high with a big account one week and lose it the next, without ever knowing quite what hit. Fremerman Papin certainly contributed to my education.

One incident I remember with pride. The agency was interested in landing political accounts, and we had our eye on the up-and-coming young congressman from northwest Missouri, Jerry Litton. In the middle 1970s he was laying plans to run for the Democratic nomination for the U.S. Senate. Many ad agencies vied for the account, and so did we. Marvin Fremerman, Bernie Papin and I took Litton to lunch at Bretton's and made our pitch. Litton was impressed but thought our price was too high. He said he'd keep looking. As we were walking back to our office in the Kansas City Power & Light Building — Litton and I trailing the two partners by several paces — I had an inspiration. Turning to Litton, I said:

"Jerry, you're rich, aren't you? I understand that you could probably afford an agency like ours where some could not. The thing we can do for you is begin work for you this afternoon. How many of your opponents could start that soon? And you would be in good hands."

Just before we got to 14th Street, Litton said: "You know, you're right, I'm going with you guys."

I walked up to the partners and said, "Gentlemen, Jerry has changed his mind and is coming with us. I told him we could start work on his campaign this very day." They both looked astonished, but go to work we did — that afternoon.

"What happened?" Bernie Papin said after Litton had left. "What did you say to him?"

"I just decided since all was lost I might as well make a bold play," I replied. It was exciting to land this account and it also told me something that I hadn't known—that I was a pretty fair salesman. I loved seeing the big smile on the face of my friend, Bernie Papin.

INTERLUDE

On Hosting a Talk Show

A lot of what's done in broadcasting is pretty routine, but not always on a talk show. With every caller there's a potential risk in what they might say, so your adrenaline is working the whole time.

Want to become a talk-show host? Do you have your heart set on it? First, you might check with a therapist, but if you still aspire to doing it, here are some things to bear in mind.

The difficult guest

Some talk shows operate only with hosts, hoping each day that the switchboard fills up with calls. That format is popular on AM radio. Other shows bring guests into the mix, but that can be hazardous. If you, as host, or your producer carelessly books a really rotten guest, you're stuck.

An example of the breed is a guest you thought had interesting views or expertise. But put him or her on the air and they fall apart like a cheap suit. Now, do you hang in there and keep trying to make something out of the show, or politely dismiss the guest? If it's the latter, you're faced with a new problem. You may discover that, having kept the bad guest on too long, you've driven away your usual audience. That's when the crazies begin calling. This brand of caller, a reject on any healthy talk show, includes the political fanatic, the religious extremist, the faith healer, the person who wants to talk dirty, and the ones whose messages are merely gibberish. They know you need them to fill air time and they take full advantage of it. This is avoidable if you think carefully about the guests you choose and their ability to talk entertainingly — or at least informatively.

The guest with a teacher complex

You are going to have a long, dreary hour if you ask your guest several questions and the answer each time is, "That is correct." After you've heard "That is correct" the third time, stop the show dead in its tracks and say, "Listen, this is a talk show; are we going to have a conversation or are you grading papers?" If the guest persists, it is correct for you to get rid of them.

Open line and open mike

On these shows the host acts as oracle and feels ready to answer questions about anything. Too often, "open mike" hosts are put-down artists, and their audiences are filled with folks spoiling for a fight. Better is a "listener line," in which the host or producer picks out and prepares several timely questions to put to the audience.

Undercover audiences

WHB management assumed that by changing from Top 40 to grown-up programming at 10 p.m. its most important customers, kids, would either tune out or go to sleep. Apparently every night, hundreds and maybe thousands of kids told to go to bed at 10 p.m. instead would go to their rooms, slip under the covers with a transistor radio and listen to "Nightbeat." At the time I didn't know that they were out there but now, years later, I hear repeatedly from middle-age people who once did just that. "Nightbeat" had a large undercover audience!

Guest abuse

Occasionally a caller simply wants to publicly embarrass a guest. As a rule, anonymity is granted to callers so they can speak frankly and freely, but when they hide behind it so they can harm someone on the air, my policy is to break in. "Before you go any further with this," I'll say, "you've gone beyond just criticizing and are now into personal attacks. This guest came on the air fully identified and took the chance of receiving any kind of call. If you want to continue this you must identify *yourself*." Upon hearing that, the caller usually hangs up.

A few, however, don't give up so easily. One night on WHB's "Town Hall" local TV anchorman John Masterman was our guest. Everything was moving along smoothly, until all of a sudden we got a call from someone who clearly did not like him. Their conversation grew hot and then hotter.

"I ought to punch you out," the caller shouted.

"Well, the show ends at midnight," Masterman replied, "and we're in the Power & Light building downtown. Come on down if you're so eager."

We continued with the show, wrapped it up and rode down the elevator together. Imagine our surprise when John and I got off the elevator and there stood a man who looked to be about half Masterman's size. He announced that he was our feisty caller. Masterman recognized that it wouldn't do for a public figure like himself to get into a public fight — particularly not with someone much smaller. So he put his arm around his antagonist.

"I'm sorry I made you unhappy," Masterman told him. "Let's just be friends and let it go. I don't want to hit you and I don't think you want to hit me."

Everybody agreed and we all went in peace.

Variety is the spice of a talk show

There is an old show-business saying, "Never follow one banjo act with another banjo act." Never cover the same subject twice in a week.

Faith and good works rarely make a good talk show.

If there is no controversy, no deep human interest, and no humor that can bring on good conversation, you are dead in the water. A show that covers only the great works of an organization or individual will not find or hold an audience. You have to tell the lady who wants to get her preacher on the air, and the people who are devoting their lives to making the world a better place, that what they do is wonderful but unlikely to produce many calls.

Avoid booking your closest friends.

Invariably they will get into inside stories or humor, which do nothing for the audience and slow down the show. There are those who feel they're on intimate terms with you, and begin to act familiar —

referring to personal stories that you've shared. Either way, there's nothing duller than stories no one else knows anything about.

Passing away or passing out

The worst thing I ever heard of happening on a talk show beset the smooth and polished Dick Cavett. As Cavett chatted with another guest, publisher and organic-food advocate Jerome I. Rodale lowered his head to his chest and died on stage. Rodale, then 72, had recently boasted that he would live to be 100 years old. The show was never broadcast. The next worst thing to having a dead guest on your show would be to have a dead drunk. Once or twice in my career, I've had a guest who looked just fine until they sat down and began to talk. That's why most good talk shows want guests to arrive 15 to 30 minutes before airtime.

Presidents

Richard Nixon

One day in summer 1971 President Nixon, no doubt feeling embattled by the Washington press corps, made an appearance before about 150 Midwestern broadcast and newspaper executives in Kansas City. With that group in that setting, perhaps, he might meet more open hearts and minds. He spoke at the Holiday Inn downtown, in a square room on the lower floor of the hotel. The chairs were arranged so the president could follow a diagonal path, lined with red carpet, to the speaker's stand. The idea, apparently, was that the president could stride straight to the platform.

Nixon was one of those speakers who liked to fix his eyes on friendly faces in the audience. He selected one friendly face on the left side of the room, one in the middle and finally one on the right, and rotated his gaze as he spoke. Many of the editors and news directors gave him a lot of positive attention and he spoke on and on. The length of the president's comments — about 40 minutes — and the warmth of the full room made me drowsy and I fell asleep briefly. Awakening, I was met by the disbelieving look of the president of the United States talking directly to me. Mine was the friendly face on the president's left. Surely I had made the enemies list!

There was a reception afterward upstairs. We all attended and shook hands with various dignitaries, including Richard Helms, director of the CIA, who seemed like a friendly enough chap. I joined the reception line, fully intending to confront the president about ending the war in Vietnam.

I imagined what I would say: "Mr. President, four years from now, you won't be able to get any

Interviewing dignitaries and spouses at the opening of the Auditorium Plaza Garage in 1955.

With Harry S. Truman and Randall Jessee, left, in the WDAF newsroom.

Writing copy at WDAF.

With Robert F. Kennedy and my co-host Jean Glenn on "Conversation," at Bretton's Restaurant.

He didn't have much to say, but Rock Hudson drew a crowd for his appearance on "Conversation" at Bretton's.

A good sport, Kennedy press secretary Pierre Sallinger after receiving his award from the Kansas City Press Club. I'm on the left and Jean is on the right.

On "Insight," a television interview program, Bill Leeds and I interviewed Thomas Hart Benton and scores of other celebrities.

With Chet Huntley, center, on "Insight."

At my post at WHB.

Behind the mike at KMBZ for my nightly talk show.

Teaching my twice-a-week class at the University of Missouri-Kansas City, 1992.

Relaxing at Southmoreland Park near the Nelson-Atkins museum, mid-1990s.

Broadcasting "The Walt Bodine Show," on KCUR.

more concessions than you are getting now. If you settle now, a lot of lives could be saved, so why don't you end it now?"

Gradually I worked my way to the front of the line, where a tall man in a military uniform leaned forward and said, "Name, please."

"Bodine," I told him. He leaned over just as the previous person in line was moving away and as I was moving up, and I saw him whisper to the president. The president of the United States then greeted me and said in a deep, rich voice, "I'm glad to meet you Mr. Bodine." Suddenly my speech about ending the war in Vietnam evaporated. That daring reporter who was going to confront him about the war instead was saying: "Mr. President, it's nice to have you in our city. You must come see us more often."

I slunk off into a corner, ashamed of my lack of courage but consoled by the fact that there was little chance he'd call off the war in Vietnam on my say-so. It ended with the eating of hors d'oeuvres. The president and his entourage went on to San Clemente, California, and the rest of us made it back to our wholesome lives in the heartland.

*   *   *

Nixon unknowingly created an awkward

moment at the Truman Library in Independence
when he stopped in town to present a piano that had
been in a section of the presidential study in
Truman's term. Truman had played it, as had his
daughter, Margaret. Maybe Nixon was trying to woo
this part of the country, or Mr. Truman, but the effort
backfired when he sat down at the piano and played
"Missouri Waltz" for the former president. Unaware
that Harry Truman had grown sick and tired of
"Missouri Waltz" after hearing it played over and
over in his 1948 election campaign, Nixon had a sly
smile on his face as he played, perhaps contemplating
what he thought was a public-relations coup. No
doubt, Truman continued sincerely to hate his guts.

*   *   *

I crossed paths with Nixon several more times
— at political conventions, and when he came to
town to announce that he was naming Kansas City's
police chief, Clarence Kelly, head of the FBI. Yet the
oddest occasion was one visit when the presidential
limousine drove down 12th street, turned south on
Wyandotte and stopped at the entrance on the west
side of the Muehlebach Hotel. The president was
expected to get out on the sidewalk, but instead he
emerged on the Wyandotte Street side and headed
straight for the park atop the Auditorium Plaza

Parking Garage. Apparently, he thought it might be an interesting touch to go shake a few hands. As he entered the park, leaving the Secret Service temporarily behind, I walked along parallel to him about a dozen feet away. In those days, the little park was not the Barney Allis Plaza of today, and the president encountered mostly empty whisky bottles and people sleeping on benches. He turned on his heel and headed back for the Muehlebach. By then the Secret Service agents realized what had happened, rushed to surround the president and re-establish their territory. I was walking some distance from Nixon as the scene played out, yet a Secret Service agent rushed up and elbowed me. I fell and the blow cost me a sprained ankle and a week on crutches. Evidently, the agent was trying to make sure everyone knew which territory was his.

CHAPTER VII

KMBZ Night Talker - Dodging Baseballs - Alligator Man - KMBC -
Lovable Joints - Bowl of Chili and a Malted - Mel at the Diner -
Derring-Do on Suicide Hill - Goodbye to Television

T here it was, 20 feet tall, staring at me from beside the
freeway — my own face. It looked at me from a giant
billboard, and emblazoned over it were the words, "Master of
Night Talk." That's how KMBZ boomed me, its new, nighttime
talk-show host in a new program, "The Walt Bodine Show."

KMBZ's general manager, Walt Lochman, had read the
ratings books and seen that "Sunday Town Hall" on WHB was
doing well. In 1978 he offered me more money and a deal was
done. For the next four years, I would be the Master of Night Talk
at a new address, 980 on the AM dial.

I hadn't known Lochman well, but we had a lot in common.
We were both Walts; in fact we were both Waltons.
Coincidentally, we spent our boyhoods in the same home at
different times. His father was a well-known play-by-play sports
announcer who rented an English bungalow owned by my father
on 75th Street in the Waldo area. My family had lived there briefly
in the 1930s, right after it was built. Yet in all the time we had both
spent in broadcasting, we'd never met face-to-face until the late
1970s.

Our first encounter came when he asked whether I'd write occasional editorials for KMBZ. One of the station's concerns was that despite high ratings its audience skewed toward male and middle-age listeners. I wrote an editorial supporting the Equal Rights Amendment, the station's editorial board approved it and it aired six or seven times a day for two days. KMBZ was owned by the Mormon church and, as a matter of course, editorials were mailed to Salt Lake City every week. One night, I received a phone call at home from Walt Lochman's secretary, Patty Finkle.

"A mushroom cloud went up over Temple Square in Salt Lake City today," she said wryly, explaining that a high official in the church had just read my editorial and exploded. I was saved through the good graces of Walt Lochman, who made the case that I was new on the job. I survived to write another day. Finally in July 1978 the talk-show slot came around.

As Master of Night Talk I spent summers dodging in and out with the Kansas City Royals baseball games. In those years the Royals were immensely successful and immensely popular, and they were a staple on KMBZ. On the other hand, I never knew from night to night whether I'd have a show or not, depending on whether a game went into extra innings. Or the opposite could happen. The game could be wiped out by rain and "The Walt Bodine Show" would expand to an entire evening. It would continue until 11:30 p.m., when a paid religious program began. If the ballgame ran long, getting closer to the preacher's time, there might be a gap of 20 minutes or less. I was expected to fill it with a mini-talk show. On most such nights I had a guest or two who sat around with me watching the clock, listening to sports, and watching their time drain away. You knew they were thinking, "When, if ever, does this show go on?"

KMBZ was, indeed, focused on sports. There was always a pre-game show, a show with the Royals' manager, the ballgame itself, and afterward a station break and then back to the ballpark where the play-by-play men summarized what you had just heard and read scores from other games. After more commercials, Don Burley came on. I fielded the questions from the sports fans, relaying callers' questions to Burley. After a while people would begin to think that I, too, was a baseball expert and they would call and ask a question for which — believe me! — I had no answer. I learned to say, "Well Don and I were talking about that just the other day — weren't we, Don? — and you had a great way of summing it up...."

Each night while the game was under way, I worked in the studio putting together future shows. Because I'm not a sports fan I never consciously listened to a game, yet by the end of each season I knew the names of every player, the record of the team and what was happening with managers around baseball. All of it just seemed to seep into my consciousness. Don't get me wrong; I know it's great for a town to have a major-league team. Once every two or three years I'd take my kids to the ballgame and enjoy it. However, they didn't understand my theory of attending ballgames — that the higher up you sat the less you'd be bothered by the game and the more you could concentrate on eating a hot dog and drinking a beer.

Despite the problems in baseball season, the show had its moments. One night my featured guest was Lawrence Welk, who told me: "This is the pinnacle of my career. I've always wanted to be on this talk show and I thank you for booking me in."

Sure, he was putting me on — some might say big time — but what could I do? It's hard to call a man a liar who has just said how much he likes you. I did spit out, "Are you conning me or what?" Right away, Welk glanced at Cindy Monaco, the producer, who was a college student, a ballet dancer and pretty.

"Couldn't we put on a little music?" he asked. "Come in here, producer, come on in here." She put on a tune, entered the studio and she and Welk danced around. I did the play-by-play. Next time you are at a dance imagine what it's like to describe two people dancing.

It always seemed that the tuba was a vital instrument in an orchestra, but that tuba players got little recognition. One night I announced that I'd like to get some tuba players on the air playing their instruments. The next night 11 of them showed up, filling the studio and playing together. There was no lack of "oom-pah-pahs." What a sound!

"The Walt Bodine Show" also featured a parade of mishaps. Once, a public-relations person of questionable intelligence told us about a Buddhist monk who was walking from coast to coast through the United States to promote peace. The monk was to be in town on a Wednesday night and we could have him at 7 p.m. if we wanted him. Fine, I replied. What the agent didn't mention, and maybe didn't know, is that the man apparently had taken a vow of silence.

As that night's show began, I introduced the monk and waited for him to say something. He just smiled and gave a little bow.

"Perhaps we have a little problem with language here," I said. "I guess you're having a long, long walk."

Yes, he nodded.

Did his feet hurt?

Yes, he nodded.

Finally we went to a station break and I called in the producer.

"Would you escort this man back out?" I said, "Thank him for being here — and let me know if he answers you." The monk smiled all the way to the door and clutched his hands together and gave a little bow as he left. On the radio, a person like that is about as useful as a Boy Scout demonstrating semaphore signals.

Once in a while a genuine nut dropped in. One night I was interviewing service people who had spent time in Vietnam, talking about the psychological repercussions of their experience, when a man with a burr haircut appeared at the station door wearing what looked like Army fatigues. He walked into the control room, announced that he was a medal of honor winner, called my guests a bunch of wimps, and demanded to talk on the air. The engineer engaged him in conversation while the producer made her way to the studio. One of our guests was a psychologist, so I whispered the problem to him and suggested he take our uninvited guest down the hall to calm him down. The psychologist looked at me with mild alarm, but did what I asked. Shortly we heard the intruder shouting as he came back toward the studio. I told the producer to call the police if he came in. Soon, he did just that, and I said on the air, "I think we have a visitor in the studio."

I turned to the man, summoned the best story I could and said: "Sir, I have to tell you that it would be unlawful for you to come into this station and speak when you have not been invited. You're welcome to sit down there if you want to watch the rest of the show." To my relief, the man sat down on a couch. A few minutes later the police came in, recognized him and told us he was not a medal of honor winner, but someone who got out of control once in a while. The last time he had been picked up was for directing traffic in the middle of Rainbow Boulevard at Shawnee Mission Parkway.

One night an animal lover brought in a small alligator. He sat down beside me, holding the alligator as you'd hold a baby, telling me I had nothing to fear. A minute later the animal lunged at me and I moved my microphone and myself to get more distance. The animal's handler, as I recall, said he was sure the alligator was confused by the lights.

My talk show originated from a large studio just across the hall from a second studio housing KMBR, which had a beautiful-music format. The announcer, Roberta Solomon, didn't have much to do because the show was largely automated. One night she said: "Guess what! I've landed a gig. I'll be the hostess of a creature feature on Channel 41. They asked me to think of a name for myself. How does Crematia grab you?" I said: "Just fine. Have you got a last name yet?" She said, "No." And I said, "How about Mortem?" Thus Crematia Mortem was born on the local media scene and her show, which was directed by Rob Forsythe, reigned for several years. It was a favorite with kids — and with more adults than cared to admit it.

Walt Lochman was fun to work with, performed at high energy the whole workday, and loved a good idea when he heard one. But he could also fall in love with a bad idea, and that proved my undoing at KMBZ. One day I learned from Steve Bell, the program director, that Lochman had decided to experiment with stereo AM radio at night, when stations could afford to try different things. In late 1982 the ax fell on me. In place of "The Walt Bodine Show," they would try out a disc jockey on AM stereo radio. KMBZ would be the first in town. As far as I know, there never was a second.

One day in 1982 a letter arrived from Michael Sullivan, the Number Two man at Channel 9 news, asking to get together. I met with him and Pat McCarthy, the news director. McCarthy said that the newsroom needed a commentator with deep experience in the community. He had my undivided attention.

"I think you could do this," he said. "How much time would you need every day? Five minutes?"

Way too much, I said, adding: "I come from the school in which commentary should be brief and to the point. One minute is plenty — two minutes for something large."

We compromised on one and a quarter minutes if the story could be told quickly and, if not, two minutes maximum. I would be on the air Monday through Friday and could do commentary on whatever I wanted. I could be lighthearted as well as serious. With that we set times and dates and money, and for several years I did TV commentary five days a week.

I was still appearing on Channel 41, writing editorials for KMBZ radio and teaching a broadcast journalism course two days a week at the University of Missouri-Kansas City. Why add more to that load? I was raised a child of the Depression, and I can remember what a catastrophe it was when anyone in the family lost a job. Probably I went to the other extreme, making sure I always kept many irons in the fire.

But the daily TV commentaries eventually became a drag, and I told McCarthy and Sullivan, "You know, there are guys who have an opinion every two hours and there are other guys who are slow to form an opinion, and I'm one of them."

At my age, I was finding that there were a lot of things that I simply was uncertain about. I took very seriously the saying that it's not what you don't know that will hurt you, it's what you know for sure that isn't so.

I wanted to do human pieces, maybe some local color. I heard that Kent Replogle, the general manager at the time of my hiring, was willing to let the news department do that but cautioned, "Television has left Bodine behind." A few weeks later, he sent word that he thought I was going to do just fine.

As luck would have it, only a day or two later I heard about the closing of a much-loved neighborhood bar on Main Street south of the Country Club Plaza. It was called A Street Car Named Desire, complete with the shell of an old interurban car in the front. You entered through the streetcar; the main part of the bar was inside an old house. On closing day, I arrived with a camera crew and shot a piece just sitting at the bar talking to the people, picking up the sound of "Auld Lang Syne." Folks were getting bluesy and bit woozy. It was a thoroughly urban scene — the old and beloved and slightly run down giving way to the sleek high-rise office building soon to take its place. The piece struck a note with Sullivan, who by then had become news director.

"This is something you can do," he told me. "You called it a lovable joint. You know the town; why don't you visit other lovable joints and tell us about them and the people who go there?"

"Bars mostly?" I said.

"Bars and other places that people are attached to."

He suggested I cover mostly mom-and-pop diners and restaurants with blue-plate specials and changing menus and a loyal following.

One day I was out with KMBC's promotion person shooting promos for my feature on the 6 o'clock news. As we parted company she said, "You know what your signoff is going to be?"

"No, got an idea?" I said.

"Sure, you say it all the time: *'What do you say to that?'*"

We added a visual consisting mostly of my signature after the words, "What do you say to that?" and that's how I ended every segment. At various times my piece appeared on the 5 o'clock, the 6 o'clock and, once in a great while, the 10 o'clock news.

In my nearly 18 years with KMBC the format changed often. We aired "Budget Banquets" during a recession. "One of a Kind" described the Kansas Citians who were undeniably one of a kind — the Alligator Lady, the Crusading Bartender, the Mouse Man (he raced mice on a miniature track in his backyard), Lamar the Doughnut King, and the Split-Personality Waitress.

One winter, we headed out to "Suicide Hill" on Brookside Boulevard, which comes to life after a snowfall. Kids gather with their sleds to race down the hill. I decided it would make a great show to ride a sled down the hill while describing it. The day we went the temperature was hovering just above zero, so I wanted to finish as fast as possible. I gave one kid a buck to let me ride the sled down with him toward the camera. We did and I talked into the mike as we zoomed along. Then we hit a large rock underneath the snow. The sled flew up into the air, turned over and we both landed face down in the snow.

"That's enough of this for today," I said, standing up. With my usual sign-off — "What do you say to that?" — I saw Pam Klugh, the photographer, doubled over in laughter.

"I'm freezing to death," I said to her. "Let's go."

"I'm sorry," Pam said, "but that was so funny and I was laughing so hard I missed it. We're going to have to do it again."

I gave her a stern look and said: "Get it this time. I may not last for a third one." I went up to the top of the hill again and found the same kid and said: "I'll give you two bucks this time. Head straight for the camera and look out for the rock." We came down in fine style except once again the kid failed to notice where the rock was, and once again we went sailing through the air, and landed face down in the snow. I rarely watched myself on the news but that night I wanted to see how this one turned out. What I enjoyed the most was Brenda Williams, the anchor that night, turning to Len Dawson and saying, "I can't believe he did that." I felt like a hero for just one show.

What caught on were my reviews of eateries. Often I'd be walking on the Plaza, or downtown, or Brookside and someone would call out as they drove past, "Hey, Walt, where are you going to have dinner tonight?" or "Where's a great place to get a good bowl of chili?" I can't recall getting a piece of mail that didn't end with, "What do you say to that?"

Once I was on a shoot at 11th and Broadway with Tim Twyman, a photographer at Channel 9, and we had to start over a dozen times. People kept driving by and yelling, "Hey, what do you say to that?" or "What's for dinner tonight?" or "Where's the best hamburger?" On the umpteenth try I thought we had it. The traffic was falling just right and I was standing talking to the camera and almost finished when I heard a voice:

"Hey, mister, is this Broadway?"

Surely she's talking to someone else, I thought, and just kept going.

Again: "Hey, mister! Mister! Is this Broadway?"

I stopped, turned around and said, "Yes, ma'am, this is Broadway. That's why it says so on that sign there," pointing to the street sign above us. I turned around and said to Tim, "Do we have the nerve to do this again?" We did and we made it.

I can't tell you how many times restaurant owners have said to me, "Gosh, I just can't get good help anymore." If you are a regular restaurant-goer, you may notice that Restaurant A has new help every time you go in, and Restaurant B has a consistent corps of servers. Perhaps that's because tips are better in one restaurant than another, but it might also be that servers are treated better in one place. If employees are treated like professionals they'll behave like professionals. I've learned to have a great deal of regard both for the staff and for the people who own and operate restaurants.

What kind of guy doesn't like chicken? Fried chicken, um-m-m-m, wonderful! Roast chicken! Any kind of chicken! For that matter, what kind of guy doesn't care for seafood? What kind of guy would skip any banquet for a good bowl of chili with a malt and maybe a hot dog on the side? What kind of guy passes up the most expensive, most exquisite French wines in favor of a Bloody Mary with a shot of draft beer? What kind of guy doesn't eat lamb because he doesn't like to eat anything that is soft, curly and goes "bah-h-h?"

Answer: me.

It's true. I'm a finicky eater — maybe even a neurotic one.

That's why I've never presented myself as a food or restaurant "critic," but simply as a guy who tries things out. At least once a year in my time at KMBC, I issued a disclaimer owning up to all of my food peculiarities. I didn't know the names or the ingredients, much less the spelling, of exotic French sauces. But I could take viewers to hundreds of interesting places — particularly if they served comfort food.

We never filmed a restaurant without trying it beforehand, sometimes two or three times. Gourmet friends often went along, and sometimes I used their opinions. After all, there were all those foods I don't like. I limited my expertise to chili and barbecue, roast beef in a lot of variations and soda-fountain items. My idea of a perfect meal is a bowl of Town Topic chili and a chocolate malt.

For many of the shows about lovable joints, I was seated at a table describing the four or five dishes the restaurant had set out. Sometimes, the owner got carried away and put a dozen or so items at the table and we'd have to tell him that less is more. We had only one minute to describe the joint and show its food.

One piece stands out in my mind. Remember the TV show, "Alice" with Mel running the diner? Mel was played by the late Vic Tayback, who was doing a stage show in Kansas City when I arranged with him to come out to Sanderson's at 38th and Main. In the cloakroom he changed into his Mel getup of white T-shirt, apron and cap. We put a camera on Tayback and another on the customers. On cue, Tayback came bursting through the door and shouted to the waitresses: "How many times have I told you girls, no personal calls on the phone! Come on, get rid of that call and let's get going!"

Another camera cut to the customers for their reaction.

One asked, "What are you doing?" Tayback replied, "I just bought this joint and I'm going to straighten it out!" A cab driver at the counter had started to lift a cup of coffee to his lips when "Mel" burst in. His eyes widened and then as Tayback went back and forth behind the counter, you could see the cabbie turning and watching while his hand holding the coffee cup froze in mid-air.

Channel 9's photographers were creative folks and often made suggestions that made the difference between an OK piece and a great piece. As my vision diminished, they were also good at escorting me around. As soon as I hopped out of a Channel 9 truck, a photographer would come alongside and offer his or her right elbow. The key to managing my blindness is to hold lightly to someone's right elbow so I can sense when they're stepping up and down, or turning. I'll never be able to thank all of those wonderful photographers enough for looking out for me. The same goes for Channel 9 street reporters, among them Brenda Washington, formerly one of my students at UMKC, Maria Antonia, Bev Chapman, and Kris Ketz.

Television had always been exciting, particularly when I was on the news side and we were working on a big, breaking story. But as time went on, my experiences in TV began to change. Eventually, my pieces were moved to the weekend. A succession of young producers seemed a bit mystified with how to handle them. The bell, I could see, was tolling.

There had been changes in management and structure at KMBC and it looked as if I wasn't going to fit the new mold. My restaurant pieces didn't especially amuse the young producers — and in turn the young producers didn't amuse me much. In a way, though, I can sympathize with them. Set-ups in restaurants weren't exciting. I'd sit at a table behind plates of food and they would get a shot of that, and of the kitchen or the general décor. It was wearing thin and besides, television is attracted to the young and beautiful. What could it do with this old guy?

Early in 2001 I said my goodbyes to Channel 9 and to its wonderful assignment editors, especially Brenda Poor, who later moved to Channel 5. It was one of the finest news staffs I'd ever worked with.

INTERLUDE

Pols Who Kept the Pot Boiling

The city charter of Kansas City, Missouri, makes sure that nobody — particularly the mayor — holds any real power. Some regard our rather odd system as a virtue, figuring powerless politicians won't be able to do much damage. I believe it is a fault. It takes power to make things happen.

Among those who've filled the mayor's office since the downfall of the Pendergast regime in 1940 have been several I like to call The Respectables. John B. Gage, William Kemp, Ilus W. Davis and Richard Berkley all were gentlemen to a fault — namely, they didn't raise much hell. They formed a long gray line. Far more interesting to me were other mayors, each of whom had gentlemanly qualities but whose public persona was far more intriguing than any of The Respectables.

H. Roe Bartle

This giant man knew what a bully pulpit was

and how to use it. Bartle, overweight on a truly
grand scale, had a voice that could override a rock
band and a fine sense of showmanship. In the City
Council chamber he added humor and life to
otherwise dull proceedings. He had a running
conversation with one City Council member in
particular, Harry Davis, who continually referred to
Bartle as "your worship." That, I imagine,
scandalized some of the proper City Council
members and some of the public, but it delighted
Bartle.

It was a special treat to watch the mayor close
out a long, drab council session. Someone would
move to adjourn, Bartle would announce that the
motion had passed and raise an enormous gavel into
the air. As he brought the gavel crashing down, he'd
proclaim "And may peace and harmony reign
supreme..." Boom! It was refreshing —the big noise
by the big man, just to wind up one more session of
the council.

Bartle's flair for showmanship carried over to
the streets. On a hot summer night, he would crawl
into the front seat of the mayor's limousine beside
the policeman who drove him. In the back seat
would be a white fireman's hat with a big Number
One and the words, "The Chief." Around City Hall,
that was how people referred to Bartle. If a major fire
broke out while the mayor was in his limousine,

Bartle would put on the fireman's hat and his driver would rush him to the scene. Sometimes, the limousine would pull up along a sidewalk, its windows rolled down, while the mayor waited for something to happen on the police or fire department radios. He would chat with passersby. Only out-of-towners wondered who this giant man with the gigantic voice was, sitting at curbside.

At WDAF one day, H. Roe Bartle appeared for a roundtable discussion, a format that used to flourish on the radio and passed for public service. Five or so people sat around the table in a big studio, all speaking into what some call a salt-shaker microphone that could pick up voices from all sides. The only problem was that The Chief could be heard all too well. Engineers went crazy trying to even out the mayor's voice, which boomed into the mike at least 10 times louder than that of the others around the table. Finally someone got the nerve to ask Bartle to move his chair back four or five feet. Even then, his voice still nearly overpowered the rest.

As a young reporter I was nervy enough once to ask him his weight. He simply smiled and said, "Let's talk about something else." Once at a party hosted by the late Judge Henry Riederer, the guests were gathered in a large front room when Mrs. Riederer said, "Oh, my goodness, let's get ready; here comes the mayor." Immediately, people familiar with the mayor's girth and sitting needs brought out two chairs and placed them side-by-side, one for each buttock. This was a man who would always introduce his wife, Margaret, a trim and attractive woman, as "my child bride." She was a good sport and always gave a big smile.

Bartle served many years as an executive of the Boy Scouts of America in our region. The enormous man in his Scout uniform made a startling sight.

Bartle had a special talent for finding things in what looked like a disorderly stack of newspapers and other papers piled on a large table behind his swivel chair. You might say, "Mayor, what about that report on street resurfacing in the South Side?" He'd whirl around in his chair, regard the stack of papers for a moment, reach into it and pluck out the very item you were talking about.

Charles Wheeler

Another mayor who easily attracted public attention was Charlie Wheeler, doctor of medicine, doctor of law.

As mayor, Wheeler had a sense of showmanship and a sense of humor, and they often combined. Hanging on the walls of the mayor's office were hats he had collected from many of his visitors. When he sat down behind his big desk on the 29th floor of City Hall, you could tell he enjoyed the job.

Wheeler conducted regular weekly news conferences that were as unpredictable as the man himself. Reporters filed in to his office, cameras were set up, and lights were adjusted. Whenever things got interesting the television stations' lights went on, and with Wheeler the photographers had to stay on their toes because things could change any second. Sometimes Wheeler would come on with a mundane guest, perhaps a city department head. Other times he'd bring in a personage from far away who happened to be visiting City Hall. Out of courtesy, the reporters would ask the visitor a question or two. Wheeler might ramble on for a while and all of a sudden — wham! — drop a real news story. Quickly, the TV lights went on, all the reporters straightened up in their chairs and began to take note.

As mayor, Wheeler was always affable, but did not suffer fools gladly. Once a brand-new reporter just hired by one of the AM stations was taking part for the first time in the press-conference ritual. He watched the banter go back and forth, and he didn't seem to approve. Just as the session was about to end, Wheeler asked for questions, and the new reporter stood up. In a demanding tone he asked, "Mr. Mayor, I would like to know when we're going to get cable television in this town." With only a brief pause Wheeler looked at him and said, "Thursday."

Everybody laughed and the meeting came to an end.

One day I was talking with the mayor and some other men over lunch at the Rockhill Club bar. A man walked in, gasped and collapsed. Wheeler, a pathologist, dashed over, slid down and put the victim's head on his knee to keep him from swallowing his tongue. A call went out for another doctor and a second physician came over to help. The ambulance arrived shortly and took the man away. When Wheeler returned to the table I remarked that I had never seen anyone go to a sick person's aid so swiftly.

"Well, gentlemen," Wheeler said, "just remember this: If you ever have a stroke or a seizure, pray to God you get something better when they ask for a doctor in the house than one pathologist and one dermatologist."

He appeared regularly on Mike Murphy's show when Murphy was a morning disc jockey. Wheeler had written a book called *Doctor in Politics*, and in one of those brief encounters with Murphy he said, "By the way, Mike, have you read my book?"

"Mayor," Murphy said, "I picked it up, I read quite a bit of it and then I had to do something else and I put it down. You've written the kind of book that if you lay it down, you can't ever pick it up again!"

Emanuel Cleaver

Another who broke the mold of The Respectables was the Rev. Emanuel Cleaver, affectionately known to the press and others as "The Rev," who had a rare gift of getting people to listen to his ideas and of making things happen. Like Wheeler, Cleaver has a quick sense of humor. I listened to him one time when he was performing a wedding on his Friday show on KCUR radio. He went through the usual phrases a preacher says at a wedding and then he came to the line that traditionally goes, "If any man knows a reason why this couple should not be joined in holy wedlock, let him speak now or forever hold his peace."

"The Rev" shortened it to, "If anyone knows a reason why this couple should not be joined in holy wedlock, what are you doing here?"

Kay Barnes

In her regular visits on KCUR she has been a pleasant personality, but in the beginning she'd too often answer questions from the public by advising the caller to get in touch with her office. After a few instances of that, I asked the mayor to wait a moment afterward. The show, I told her, was becoming the Call-My-Office program. In her response was a trace of irritation, but I persisted, suggesting that other political figures had brought along a trusted and well-informed aide to help with answers. From then on, the mayor brought Regina Chandler and communications improved steadily. Steadily, Mayor Barnes has grown more decisive and sure of herself in dealing with politicians, press and public.

Ever wonder what kind of advice a past mayor would give a current one? Cleaver recently was quoted as giving Mayor Barnes three bits of advice:

1. Build coalitions.
2. Build coalitions.
3. Build coalitions.

Some more tricks of the talk-show trade

The care and feeding of authors

Have the book in hand and know something about the publisher. Read it if you have the chance. Talk-show hosts are notorious for scanning books and trying to sound as if they've read them. On the other hand, touring authors are a frequent feature on talk shows and there really isn't enough time to read all the books.

Still, that's no excuse for knowing nothing. The question most hated by writers is, "So tell me, what is your book all about?" My technique is this: On the day an author is scheduled, I spend about two hours in preparation with my producer. In that time we check the Internet for reviews, read what's on the book jacket — however over-the-top it may be — and peruse the table of contents. If a chapter title sounds intriguing, we jump right to that chapter, which the producer may read aloud. Often, that raises some interesting questions. We also go over the press release that accompanies new books.

Beware of the regulars

Years ago on KMBZ radio I had a producer with a soft heart for certain listeners, the folks who call too often. "Regulars" show lots of loyalty, but you can depend on them eventually to kill a show. When a regular comes on the line, you can be sure a lot of listeners will say, "No, not that guy again," and click off or go to another station. If I had my choice of an audience composed of only the best regulars or an audience composed of strangers, I'd take the latter.

Once, while riding home with that producer one night after the show, I gave him a spiel on the subject.

"Once you've been the good guy and let some long-winded regular on the show," I told him, "then it's left to me to be the bad guy who has to get rid of them on the air with everyone listening."

Plug uglies

There's nothing worse than an out-of-control

book plugger, or for that matter anyone plugging a commercial product or commercially sponsored event. The unwritten understanding on talk shows is that in an hour program the book, product or event will be mentioned once or twice. One author was determined to plug each of the books she'd ever written. When a caller asked a simple question about how a parent should handle a specific problem, the author's answer was: "Well, you need to read my book because in my book I explain all of that." That's the time to break in and say, "I don't think it would be giving away too much to give this person more of an answer than that." When it happens, the guest usually looks startled and then tries to improve on the earlier answer.

Some callers play games. There are the restaurateurs who call, complimenting their own restaurants but trying to sound like satisfied customers. They give themselves away when they know just a little too much. They describe everything on the menu and have the hours of operation down pat. A casual customer wouldn't memorize all that. One restaurant has tried to pull that trick on us six times.

Stamp out rumors

Sometimes a caller or a guest volunteers that a certain place of business, often a competitor, is closed.

Immediately I ask: "How sure are you of this?" At least half the time the place isn't closed at all. I try to cut off rumor-mongers promptly.

Be careful of locals who made good

There's some risk in inviting a local person who has made good in the big, wide world and comes home to appear on the talk show. Some can bring this off very nicely, such as Calvin Trillin, who always provides a good show. Walter Cronkite is terrific. But too many only bring forth callers who want to make it Old Home Week. "Remember me?" the callers say. "I sat three seats behind you in Algebra in junior high." Chances are the guest will be perplexed and you'll be vexed. Once I had the late, great fan-dancer Sally Rand on WHB. She was a charming guest and very attractive, even though by then she was past society's age-limit for beauty. We were having a great conversation. Then came a call from someone who'd been her classmate at the Greenwood School on 27th Street. Sally happened to remember the caller, and they had a nostalgic conversation. But after that it seemed everyone who ever graduated from the Greenwood School called in. In those days at WHB, the talk-show host worked without a producer to screen calls. I simply picked up the phone and whoever was next was on the air. Once the Sally Rand reunion had begun, I was stuck with it.

Don't leave your show in the greenroom

In talk-show parlance the greenroom is where a guest waits to be summoned to the studio. Some nervous hosts go to the greenroom and visit at length with a guest, only to discover that all the talk has taken the spontaneity and excitement out of the broadcast that follows. On a radio show, talk is best served fresh. Worst of all is a joke shared with a host or producer beforehand, and a decision is made to repeat it on the air. Nothing is more stale than a punch line you've already heard.

Listener cliches

If I could get a message to every call-in on a talk show it would be that you don't need to:

• Thank us for taking your call. That's the purpose of the talk show. We are paid to take calls.

• Declare, "Great show today!" The show isn't great every day. Sometimes the show is just barely passable. When the show isn't very great, this line sounds phony.

• Say, "Can you hear me?" Talk shows are designed to capture and air phone calls. It's rare that we can't hear someone unless there is something wrong on their end of the line. Or they might say, "Gee, this is great, you're coming in loud and clear." We had better be or it would be a very big worry to the chief engineer. For the most part, these are well-meaning folks.

• Say, "Is that you?" Over a good part of my career I was a multi-media person working in television and radio. Because of that, people would call into a talk show and say: "Is that you? I've seen you on TV a lot." They appear to think it is a miracle to be able to talk to someone from television on the radio.

Phrases I can live without

• I do what I do (whatever it is) to "make a difference."

• "This raises more questions than it answers." Newscasters and commentators seem to love this one the most.

• "I am a people person." I thought they were a goldfish person?

• "Having said that, I would then like to say this…." Politicians love to use that one to set the stage. Why don't they just go ahead and say it?

• "I am a fiscal conservative and a social liberal." A cop-out that many use.

• "We'll just have to wait and see how this plays out…." This you get from reporters who have a beginning and a middle to a story, but no end.

• "We've got to stop meeting this way." Amateur humorists believe this is so very funny.

• "As for the outcome of all this, only time will tell." Another favorite for newscasters., who adopt a sage look while saying it.

• "If we can put a man on the moon, we can…." Just fill in the blank.

CHAPTER VIII

Going Public - KCUR - The Way We Were -
The Sweet Potato Queen -
Authors Who Know Too Little - Twenty Years in One Place

Years ago when KCUR put on its first fundraising campaign my wife, Bernie, heard the appeal on her car radio. After she got home, she told me about it and we sent in $20 each. A couple days later the telephone rang. It was Sam Scott, who had started the small public FM station at what was then the University of Kansas City and in the early 1960s became the University of Missouri-Kansas City.

"We really appreciate your donation," Scott told me. "This has been hard and we haven't pulled in much."

Sam Scott was a remarkable man who taught speech, theater and communications. Half a century ago he dreamed of creating a radio voice for the university. In 1957 Scott's dream came true and the little FM station began broadcasting in an old university building. The studio was several flights up, in a tower. It was a place where young announcers and news people could learn their trade — and where the university could extend its teaching to the whole city. When it first went on the air I could tune it in, but barely. The signal was weak even at my house only 12 blocks from campus. Sometimes, the station broadcast classroom lectures by professors wired for the radio. Those could be wonderful or terrible. The professors who walked while they talked jostled their mikes, creating distracting noise.

As general manager through KCUR's first three decades, Sam Scott fought hard for the station — often against officials high in the university administration who time and again challenged him over whether the station was necessary. They didn't think it would amount to anything, but Scott knew better.

Over the years he had asked me several times whether I was interested in moving to KCUR and in 1982, as I sniffed changes in the wind at KMBZ, I decided to talk with him. We met at Harry Starker's on the Plaza, and a deal was under way. I had taught at UMKC off and on for about a decade, and not long after my discussions with Scott, the university's Larry Ehrlich and I came to terms on my becoming a full professor in the Communications Studies Department. With everything arranged, in early 1983 the "Walt Bodine Show" opened at its new home, KCUR.

The show began in a one and one-half hour time slot weeknights, replacing classical music. In the first few weeks some of the calls in the evening were not generous; at least half the callers wanted classical music back. One night, however, Eugene Trani, who ranked high in the university administration, dropped by to say there had been a sevenfold improvement in audience. I was on sure footing.

After Patricia Cahill became the general manager in 1987, she moved the show to mornings, where the audience began to grow alongside increasingly excellent programming. It was great to be on daytime radio, where we could reach more listeners. That meant we could attract more celebrities as they came through town — authors, journalists, people from the movies and other arts.

Early in my public radio career, when fundraising time came we'd wheedle some, and threaten listeners with going off the air if they didn't donate. One night in the middle of a dreary campaign, I was working with one of the pros, Michael Davenport, who had a program called "A Little Show Music." We were trying everything, yet we couldn't seem to raise a dime. I suggested that people come close to their radios and then said, "Stick 'em up!" The money still just dribbled in.

What a contrast to today, when we invite supporters from outside the station to make the public radio pitch on the air, and dedicated volunteers take pledges. Today, fundraising is a spirited event. Each of the two campaigns we do every year brings in $200,000 to $300,000.

Aside from those pledge drives, my favorite memory of Michael Davenport was when we both were sitting in the greenroom, where performers and guests wait before going on.

"Michael," I said, glancing at his feet, "do you know that you're wearing one red sock and one white sock?"

"Yes," he replied calmly. "I'm getting older and that means I have a lot less time. Time is precious. Why should I waste it on matching socks?" Once his socks were washed and dried, he'd toss them all into one large drawer. Each day, he reached in, grabbed two socks of any color and pattern, slipped them on and forgot about the matter. The idea seemed terribly sensible to me, although I never adopted it.

One of our radio guests was a man described as the Walter Cronkite of Russia, Boris Notkin. He was a fine, good-humored man who made an engaging talk-show guest. Notkin had been visiting campus for a couple of weeks, and the faculty had wined and dined him at high-class places.

Patty Cahill passed along word that he was eager to go to an ordinary local watering hole. I jumped at the chance to take him and that night we visited Tony's on the Boulevard, a bar along Southwest Boulevard unpretentious enough to gently spoof its own name as "Antoine's" on the Boulevard. I had called in advance and told the proprietors of our guest's wish to spend a couple of hours with everyday folks. The moment we walked in we saw a sign that said, "Welcome Boris." He got a T-shirt, which he promised to wear on the streets of Moscow, and other small gifts. He was delighted.

When Ginger Rogers joined me one day at KCUR, it was the third time I had interviewed her, but a first for my producer, Kristin Van Voorst, who idolized her. The famed dancer and actress was a gracious guest. She didn't use this line on the show, but I got her to own up to saying it: she could do everything Fred Astaire could, only in high heels and backwards. As the show ended, we were preparing to take pictures at the mike. Ginger Rogers was perceptive and saw that Kristin admired her greatly. Just before they took the picture she said, "Just a minute," turned to Kristin and said, "Come over here, honey, and stand close to me." That memento made a great gift.

Judge Robert Bork appeared on the show with his wife after his failed nomination to the U.S. Supreme Court. He had encountered a tremendous amount of criticism and bad press, and I expected an angry, wild-eyed man and a lot of trouble in that hour. I was 100 percent wrong. Bork's viewpoints were, indeed, far from mine, and he was firmly literal in his interpretations of the law. Yet he turned out to be a friendly bear of a man without even a glint of radicalism in his eyes. It made a very smooth and interesting show. This large man was married to a tiny woman, a former nun, and it was clear that he adored her. Throughout the show he glanced at her and she, in turn, seemed to radiate encouragement. No matter what the differences of opinion, Bork was gracious with callers and sincere in his arguments.

On the average call-in show you'll go years before a doctor calls in. But some time back, during a discussion of health care, I saw four names on my screen. One of the names had "M.D." behind it. Then my producer checked and, sure enough, all four were doctors.

"This is the supreme moment in my life," I told the audience. "I've got four doctors in *my* waiting room."

There are recurring themes on our KCUR show. Movie critics appear every other Friday. They see the movies in private previews arranged by the distributors, not with a regular theater audience. Poor devils, they don't even get any popcorn. But they can be relied on for a lively discussion, and for guidance in moviegoing. On alternate Fridays, food critics appear and that show is guaranteed to make you hungry. When it's over we break for the door, headed for some favorite eatery.

One of our most popular formats is "Nature in the City." Despite what many city dwellers think, a tremendous assortment of animals lives among us. Some fly above us, some travel underground and some occupy the same ground we do. Joe Werner, an urban biologist, says animals seek the best possible environment and one of the biggest lures is food. Even crows are simply following their instincts. When they're flocking in your part of town, it's probably because they find food easily there. In my neighborhood, the crows used to line up about 5 p.m. across the top of the Nelson-Atkins Museum of Art — a solid row of crows making awful noises. The Nelson installed a sound effect on the roof that frightened them away, but some of them simply moved to the limb of a tree outside the window of our high-rise apartment. We think they're giving the Nelson a dirty look.

Then there's our monthly chat with Jane Flynn, a most interesting and fun historian. Jane knows her stuff and she's a careful researcher. At a listener's request she'll go to considerable lengths to find a detailed answer. Perhaps the subject is an unusual building like a castle-like house in the Northeast part of town. Or it may be the name of a street. In a format we call "As We Were," we've been able to get heavy switchboard response and great audience interest in bridges, old dance halls, and wonderful restaurants now long gone.

We got lots of reaction to an old story passed around in the Kansas City Police Department about a cop of an earlier day, when policeman wore hats like London bobbies. In those days, it didn't take much to be hired as a police officer if you didn't mind walking until your feet became flat. According to this story, an officer strolling near 25th and Bellefontaine came upon a dead horse. He took out his notebook and began to record the details: time, location and the fact that the horse was dead. He couldn't, however, spell the name of the street. There was no street marker nearby to help him, so he walked a ways and came to Agnes Street, grabbed his notebook and changed the location of the dead horse to Agnes because he could spell that.

On another show we focused on old signs. One of my favorites was downtown. It said, "Jim Kelly keeps this place, and this place keeps Jim Kelly." The most memorable sign was the famous Sherwin Williams billboard that stood facing Union Station at the bottom of Signboard Hill. It was an electric sign with lights that showed red paint pouring from a Sherwin-Williams can and covering the globe, over and over.

Once we had a guest from a travel library that sold various items for the traveler, including streetcar and bus passes for cities in Europe and Asia. I asked whether he ever got any funny questions. "On the average," he replied, "about once per month, someone will come through the door and ask if we have a globe of the United States."

I take pride in maintaining a good relationship with booksellers and book publishers. Every time you pick up a book, you're picking up a piece of someone's mind. Certain writers have become regulars on the show. I first interviewed Calvin Trillin of the *New Yorker* staff many years ago. He has been a favorite of talk-show hosts for his quick wit and his deep grasp of human nature. Richard Rhodes was a frequent visitor to KCUR. He is the Pulitzer prize-winning author of *The Making of the Atomic Bomb* and a string of other books. We did a show on every book that he wrote except one, which was just a little too naughty even for us. It was called *Making Love: An Erotic Odyssey*. Many here in his own hometown turned away from it, yet one bookseller confided to me that his store kept the book under the counter so that people had to ask for it — and ask for it they did. I'm sure Richard Rhodes will forgive me for mentioning this, just as I forgive him for stealing my producer, Ginger Untrif, to be his friend, lover and wife.

Many writers make it to a talk show only once or twice in a lifetime, and an even greater number never get on the air at all. But some I welcome back time after time, story after story. One of my favorites is a woman of both wisdom and wit, Harriet Lerner, who brought the world *The Dance of Anger, The Dance of Intimacy, The Dance of Deception* and others in an impressive series of similar titles. In each, she illustrates beautifully the realities of living and loving. Unlike Richard Rhodes and Calvin Trillin, who came from Kansas City and ended up on the East Coast, Harriet Lerner started out in New York and has settled in Kansas, most recently in Lawrence.

It's no small task to go on a book tour. Some publishers have sent people on the road for 40 straight days, one city a day, although the kinder schedulers allow the author a weekend here and there to go home and see whether they're still married and whether their children still recognize them.

Roxanne Pulitzer came through town near the end of a tour promoting her book about Palm Beach scandals, *The Prize Pulitzer: The Scandal That Rocked Palm Beach — The Real Story.* She described how she worried about the effect on her small sons of her own extensive bad publicity, and hoped they would not learn she had posed for a picture spread in *Playboy.* But one of the boys found out.

"Hey, mom," he said, "I heard at school today that you were in *Playboy.*"

She thought, "Oh, boy, now I'm trapped."

Looking him straight in the eye she said, "Yes, yes, son, I was," but before she could go any further about how she needed the money, he exclaimed, "Hey, cool!"

The worst kind of guest is the author who doesn't know much about the book he or she wrote. That happens when there's a ghostwriter who isn't along to help. Some "authors" haven't bothered, it seems, to read the book with their name on it. One recent guest was so unacquainted with the material in his book, and so inarticulate, that after only 20 minutes I thanked him for his contribution and sent him on his way. Instead of being offended, he simply looked relieved.

I do love people who have a bold creative streak. No one illustrates that better than Jill Connor Browne, who has created a one-women industry by fashioning herself into the Sweet Potato Queen. Noting that the media frequently cover the election of queens, and coming from the South, where sweet potatoes are a popular item, she declared herself Queen and made herself available for public events, parades, and other appearances. For this, she developed various kinds of *shtick* to entertain the crowds and eventually she developed books. Some folks in her hometown, Jackson, Mississippi, considered her a self-promoter. She is — perhaps the best they ever saw. She credits "The Walt Bodine Show" on KCUR for much of her success. She creates enough stir to draw a crowd almost anywhere, but when she came to Kansas City on a book tour she drew her biggest crowd by far. The next time she went out on a book tour we made sure early on that she would be welcome for another appearance on KCUR. The Sweet Potato Queen can sound very, very "country" when she wants to lay it on thick, but I also found her to be one of the smartest, surest-footed women I've ever met. She is one of my heroes, and mind you, I don't even like sweet potatoes.

I was startled recently to receive a letter from UMKC notifying me that I was eligible for a gift in appreciation of my 20 years on this job. I couldn't believe it. The time at KCUR has whizzed by and I'm ready for more. That's the great thing about talk shows — you're always ready for more because there's an endless parade of personalities. Some have jokes to tell, like Garrison Keillor. Some have had fascinating careers in news, like Walter Cronkite and Jim Lehrer. The list goes on: writers, philosophers, admirals, generals, researchers, weight-loss experts, people speaking from the depths of poverty, physicians, presidential candidates, zoo keepers, lawyers, business and computer experts, and even one astronaut.

There's not a big name every single day. But there is a big chance that you'll learn something from each guest. If the interview is handled well, you inform, amuse and sometimes astonish your listeners.

AND FINALLY ...

Thoughts on the Media

Working in both television and radio at the same time, you find yourself thinking about the virtues of each. Obviously, television can unfold dramatic moments before your eyes. Those things tend to stay with you. But when a news story lacks visual drama, radio often does better.

Some years ago I was doing a commentary in front of City Hall about a new city manager who seemed to be out of touch with his job description. He spent his time glad-handing, speechmaking and picking out furniture for his office. Bit by bit, the editorial writers and commentators began to chew away at him, and I was one of them. As Channel 9 cameras rolled, I looked up at the 29th floor of City Hall, where the city manager's office is. In this piece I said to him — albeit at a distance — "You know, you make a whole lot of money. If you just make a little trip down the hall to the men's room and back, I figured out that this would cost us approximately $14. So you might want to think about city problems while you're in there."

The fact is, he should have been thinking about city problems. I continued to describe what it would cost for him to make a personal phone call for 30 minutes, and on and on. As I continued the harangue, I shook my fist at the 29th floor.

For the next two or three weeks people came up to me to say, "I sure liked that piece you were doing in front of City Hall."

"Oh really?" I replied. "What was it about?"

"I don't know, but it was really good. You were shaking your fist and really telling them."

Another viewer: "You were really giving it to them over at City Hall, weren't you?"

"I'm so forgetful, what was I talking about anyway?"

"I don't know, but it sure was good."

Anybody who has worked very long in television has had an experience something like this, in which the picture triumphs over the content.

Radio can take that same set of facts, the heart of the story, and people will remember.

*   *   *

Broadcasters know a bad thing when they see it and they're quite willing to drag it through your living room. We hear about creeps and crazies who go bonkers and stab a few people, or take target practice at the post office or a school. Soon we begin to think everyone is going nuts. As we walk down the street we remember not to make eye contact. It's best to watch ourselves. This is a city after all. We've got to be streetwise.

Indeed, being afraid comes easily some of the time — particularly during ratings periods.

In broadcast sweeps periods, you might hear this:

"Tune in at 10 and we'll tell you how to tie your shoes. In Idaho alone, improperly tied shoes account for seven deaths a year. Forty-two were injured the same way."

Now the first thing you do in the morning is tie your shoes, so you get an early start on fear. But being afraid stays with you all day. If you get off a bus at 11 p.m., you're wary of every tree and bush. Anything may conceal an armed thug who'll demand your money, or a maniac ready to do you in just for sport.

Not to mention fearmongering on the weather. Let's say we've been enjoying a run of nice days. Then the forecaster comes on: "Enjoy it while you can. There's a storm lining up in the Arctic. By next week we'll have high winds, rain, snow." We don't even get to enjoy the weather we've got.

But what if it's been a while since it rained?

That gives us something new to worry about. Will it ever rain again?

Or there's the negative thrill. The weathercaster tells us the temperature is two degrees below zero. Just as we take that in, he robs us of the impact, saying: "This, however, is not a record. On this date in 1927 it was three below."

The scare technique works best in ads. Many a man has heard ads that ask, "Men, are you going bald?" Almost automatically their hand shoots up to their head for a quick survey of the situation. And there's Viagra. I wonder, are there men who become impotent from worrying about whether they might become impotent?

One night, I found out that people other than broadcasters were deeply interested in ratings weeks. After working later than usual, I ate dinner at the Italian Gardens and started walking back toward the television station. From a doorway someone was trying to signal me: "Pssst... pssst." It was one of the ladies of the evening and I waved to her, shook my head, and said I was on my way back to work.

"No, no," she said, "I want to ask you something." I moved a little closer to the doorway and she came out a little way to ask me whether the next week was going to be sweeps week.

"Yes," I told her.

"Do you know if they're going to do one of

those specials on prostitution?"

No, I said, I had seen the list and there were none.

"Thanks a lot," she replied. "I thought I was going to have to go to Tulsa for a week."

*　　*　　*

For too long news directors have operated on the theory, "If it bleeds, it leads." Maybe they should consider that the audience requires something more than blood and gore and sex. Can it really be that the only thing that interests us is human misbehavior? Aren't there enormous problems in the environment? Is world trade a solution to our problems or just another ploy by those seeking to dominate the world economy? Will labor unions have any role in the future? Is there any salvation for the family farm?

Emphasis put on the daily bucket of blood does nothing to answer the broad array of serious problems faced by the nation, the states and the city.

*　　*　　*

Much harm was done in commercial broadcasting when deregulation began. In many cities today, owners of broadcast properties purchase much of the broadcast market. In Kansas City one owner operates eight radio stations — all from the same building. Several of them use some of the same news personnel. Those folks must have to be cautious each time they cross the hallway to another microphone to be sure they use the right call letters.

*   *   *

When I taught a class I'd ask students what part of journalism they most wanted to enter. It depressed me to hear that more than half wanted to go into public relations. Once, when I asked them exactly what they thought PR people did, they were charmingly out of touch with reality.

"Well, you go to parties," they replied, "and you represent your company at various gatherings."

"The real answer to that," I replied, "is: You wish!"

I also asked my students where they went for news. Once again, a classroom full of young people were almost unanimous in saying CNN. A diet of CNN alone would contain precious little local news.

*   *   *

Even though it's not going to provide local news, CNN is great for an across-the-board look at the world. In fact, it has done a better job than the major networks in covering foreign news because it has more bureaus. Most of the major networks, in fact, have closed bureaus in other parts of the world.

One of the big three networks covers all of

South America from Panama City to Argentina with
one correspondent stationed in Miami. When that
correspondent goes to one of the Latin American
capitals, he or she is out of touch with day-to-day life.
That's what gives you the context of the big events.
The newly arrived reporter has to scramble to figure
out what the revolution is all about, why the
economy is falling apart, or why someone's grabbing
power.

At the networks, bean-counters have decided
they can get along on less. Years ago, William Paley
of CBS and Robert Sarnoff of NBC took pride in their
news departments. They believed that because they
were using the public's air, they owed the public
something in return. News departments weren't
even expected to run in the black; other shows would
pay their way.

Edward R. Murrow, almost a saint among news
broadcasters, began to see these trends a long time
ago. I was lucky to have been at the Blackstone Hotel
in Chicago when he delivered his speech denouncing
the money-changers in the temple of journalism.

Ronald Reagan used to speak of the "shining
city on a hill." In broadcasting there was one — once
upon a time. But it came tumbling down. I don't
know where we go from here, but I have seen hope
turn into reality before. Maybe we'll yet see
broadcasting lift its news sights somewhere beyond

profit-and-loss statements. I can only rejoice that there has been a constant growth in audiences for public radio and public television.

Bill Bates, the wonderful general manager of WDAF television and radio long ago, once told me: "I believe that if the public is offered a choice between champagne and beer they may in the long haul come to develop a champagne taste."

Cross your fingers and, in the words of Daniel Schorr, "Stay tuned...."

On Being Blind

There are a few advantages to being blind. I save on light bills, I can work in my office in total darkness, and I no longer have to match names with faces. I just ask people to identify themselves.

Back when I could see my guests, as a talk-show host I may have been subtly influenced by how people looked and by their body language. I can't make those judgments any more, and I'm glad. In a way, for me sightlessness has been a gift. These days, I come closer to taking people for what they are, rather than for what they look like. Often I ask a producer, "How old do you think that guy was?" My judgment may have been 20 years off. I'll admit that if the guest was a woman and I was impressed with what she had to say, I may ask, "What did she look like?" In general women have very nice voices, so to a blind man all women are beautiful.

When I meet a friend, I may say in the usual fashion, "You're looking great." If it's a close friend, they'll reply, "How the hell would you know?"

I still go to the movies, and occasionally I can make out shapes and figures. I usually go with a friend and sit away from others so from time to time I can ask, "What happened there?" A plot can turn on a shot from a revolver, but if you don't know who fired and who took the bullet, you're in the dark. The friend can help you out. Long silences are another challenge. Is there criminal activity or passionate lovemaking? The sounds of huffing and puffing can be the same either way.

Moviegoing is a habit I acquired early in life. When I was little, my mother played the organ accompanying silent moves at several of the larger theaters. On Friday nights she would take me with her. I'd sit in the front row and say to other guys, "Watch right there when the movie starts, and you'll see something." My mother and the huge keyboard would rise out of the pit, and the spotlight would fall on her, and I'd say: "You know what? That's my Mom."

These days I don't come away with pictures in my mind, but with thoughts or ideas. The only kind of movie I can't cope with is a foreign one with subtitles. I can't see the movie and I can't read the subtitles so there isn't much reason for me to be there — unless the popcorn is really good!

If I go to a party and talk to several people, I remember the event a day or two later through mental pictures. In my mind I assign an image to the person I talked to, including what he or she was wearing. I visualize the way the room looks. Later, when I think back about the event, I take all that for granted. Then I remember that in reality I couldn't see much of anything. On September 11, 2001, I was in front of a television a lot. When the second airliner struck the World Trade Center, I could swear that I saw the hijacked plane flying along, turning to the left and crashing into the tower.

People come to blindness in different ways, and I would never say that anything I experienced was typical. I was diagnosed with retinitis pigmentosa while I was still working at WDAF. It took almost 20 years for my eyesight to diminish to virtually nothing. Several times over the years, the decline would halt and stay on a plateau for a year or two. Maybe that's it, I would think, hopefully. I'd feel grateful if I could just retain a little vision. You know the decline has begun again when you start bumping into things, into the sides of doors of your own house, and knocking over furniture. Once I broke my toe by running into my own attaché case. I knew then that I'd lost some more ground.

When blindness happens slowly you can adapt as you go along — at least I could. I know people who've had infinitely worse experiences than mine. I can't imagine anything worse than going to bed with 20-20 vision and waking up blind. My hat is off to people who've gone through that, and still adapt and adjust.

If you've been blind for long and suddenly you were told of a new procedure to restore your sight, would you still want it back? Of course you would, most people would say. But don't be too quick to jump to that conclusion. Once you've adapted to being blind, it changes your whole way of life. Many things you thought you couldn't do without you've done without very nicely. Blindness, in fact, can encourage greater mental depth. With fewer distractions, you're able to think more deeply.

Once I had a guest who was blinded by falling into a vat of chemicals. When it happened, he was working his way through law school. After graduating, he went to work at the county courthouse, and came to know almost everyone by their voices and handshakes. One day his doctor told

him about a new procedure that could recapture his
vision. He had the operation, which was a success.
Yet readapting to seeing, he said, was every bit as
hard as losing his sight. When he first returned to
work, where everyone knew him, he couldn't match
faces to voices. Someone would come up and talk to
him in a familiar fashion, but the only way he could
recognize him or her was to close his eyes and listen
to the voice.

Even before I lost my sight, I believed people
remembered what they heard on the radio longer
than what they heard on television. Viewers can be
distracted by the kind of tie an anchor is wearing or
by the beauty of a co-anchor. Now I know it's true.

For years, I was a professor at UMKC,
preparing young people for jobs in the media and
giving them ethical perspectives on the profession.
As my eyesight diminished, it became harder to teach
because I couldn't see students' faces. Faces tell a lot
about whether you're registering with your listener.
When I first went to teach at the university I asked an
old friend, Mary Stewart, a professor of sociology,
what it took to be a good teacher. She said you must
remember that every time you walk in front of a class
it's a performance. If you can make students laugh,
or cry, or if you can frighten them, there's a good

chance they'll remember what you taught. Her
approach worked for me and I was happy when
student evaluations contained many more favorable
comments than unfavorable. As the lights went out, I
had to cut back and finally bow out of teaching.

I can't tell you how much I miss being able to
pick up a book and read it. Many people develop
the skill of reading in Braille, but I was far along in
age when my eyesight left completely, and haven't
attempted to learn that. However, more and more
books on tape are being produced. And we have the
excellent recorded books produced by the Library of
Congress and the Wolfner Library in Jefferson City.
There also has been good progress in computers that
can scan written pages and read them aloud.

One of the things I miss most is driving. From
the time I was 16, driving was something I treasured,
particularly cruising back roads and thinking things
over.

Once every month or so I dream I'm behind the
wheel of a car, usually a sports car. In one dream I'm
driving down Highway 10 to Lawrence, and in
another I'm racing through London when out of the
corner of my eye I notice a bobby who gets into his
patrol car to chase after me. In my dream, I'm
thinking, "How will I explain that I don't have a

driver's license and can't see?"   The dream ends about the time the red lights begin flashing behind me.

People wonder how I make it in a city where everyone has a car, taxi service is poor, and public transportation is nothing to brag about. It can be done — if you plan carefully days and even weeks in advance. Each weekend I try to figure ahead how I'm going to get a ride to one place, and then another, and then home. Friends and colleagues are unfailingly helpful, but every now and then I have to fall back on the philosophy espoused by Blanche DuBois in "A Streetcar Named Desire" and depend on the kindness of strangers.

That, at any rate, is how I see it. Oops, there I go again!

At any rate, I'll see you — in my dreams.